Via Mare

VIA MARE

Published by:
Arden Imprints,
17 Manchester Street,
London W1U 4DH, UK

ISBN: 1 901 268 01 2

Editor: Gillian Sutch
Editorial Consultant: Michaela Fenix
Photographer: Neil Oshima
Food Stylist: Jean-Pierre Migné
Design: Centurion Press Ltd, London
Pre Press: Rainbow Graphics, Hong Kong

Printed in Hong Kong

Via Mare

A Seafood Cookbook

GLENDA ROSALES-BARRETTO

Dear Ken,
Enjoy these recipes with a dash of your ingenuity.
With my best wishes & warm regards —
Tita Glenda
July 2001

ARDEN IMPRINTS

Contents

Foreword

I have chosen to write a foreword to this book rather than a lengthy introduction, believing that the recipes themselves will best serve to introduce my methods and ideas far better than a few hundred words could ever do. My feeling is that with cooking, as with many other skills, a 'hands on' approach is the best way of learning.

Like many of my generation, it was in my mother's kitchen that I first became aware of the joys of cooking. I recall marveling at her ability to turn a pile of raw ingredients into a delicious family meal and being overjoyed when she let me help (I wonder if that is the word that would have sprung to her mind at the time!), although little did I suspect then that this would dominate my future professional life.

My experiences since those days have introduced me to many new cuisines and culinary techniques, but those basics have always remained with me and have been the foundation on which, I like to believe, I have built a successful career and been able to delight many a discerning palate.

This is the second book of seafood recipes that I have written. The first consisted solely of Filipino dishes but in the following pages I present dishes from many different cultures gathered from my extensive travels and meetings with local cooks, both professional and domestic. I have always believed that even the best and most traditional national dishes can gain from each other and that the occasional last minute inspirational 'addition' to familiar favorites can often result in unexpected and satisfying surprises. As a result, I am always trying out new ideas.

I naturally hope that you will enjoy the recipes as I offer them but also hope that they will give you inspiration for occasionally adding to them a dash of that most important kitchen ingredient, 'cook's ingenuity'.

The oceans and rivers of the world provide a wide diversity of catches and some species found in great abundance in one place are unavailable elsewhere. If you encounter any difficulties talk to your local fishmonger. You'll find he is very knowledgeable on the subject and generally very happy to share his expertise and suggest appropriate alternatives.

HOW TO SHUCK AN OYSTER

Hold the oyster firmly with the hinge part of the shell in the palm of your hand. Push the blade between the shells.

Run the knife around the shell until you can cut the muscles that hold the valve together.

Remove the upper shell.

HOW TO CLEAN A SQUID

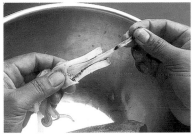

Insert your forefinger and middle finger into the squid body and pull out the head carefully.

Holding the head with one hand pull out the ink sac from the bottom but be carefull not to puncture it. Reserve ink sac for recipes that require using it.

At the top of the head, part the tentacles and squeeze the head to remove the beak from the centre. Set aside.

Hold the body with one hand and remove the plastic-like spine inside.

For the recipes that require removing the skin, hold the body with one hand and strip off the thin skin. Wash squid body and head.

HOW TO SCALE AND GUT FISH

Hold the fish firmly with one hand and scale with the other. Start from the tail and move towards the head. Wash fish to remove scales.

Hold the fish firmly on its stomach. Cut the part connecting the head and stomach.

Remove the gills from the head and the guts from the stomach. Wash the fish thoroughly inside and outside

HOW TO FILLET

Hold the fish firmly with one hand. Start cutting from the nape down to the tail.

Cut just above the tail as well as make a diagonal cut at the back of the head.

Cut the fillet from the body. Do the same procedure with the other side.

HOW TO CLEAN A FISH FILLET

Remove the remaining portion of the stomach.

Remove the skin by sliding knife starting from the tail working towards the upper part.

Wash the fillet to clean.

HOW TO CLEAN A CRAB

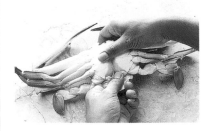

Turn the crab on its back and remove the apron.

Turn the crab again and remove the carapace.

Pull out the spongy tissue.

Remove the food sac near the big pincers.

HOW TO FLAKE A STEAMED CRAB

Remove the carapace.

Cut through the rim of the crab. This will separate the body from the claws.

Cut the body in half.

Take out the meat in lumps using a cocktail or fondue fork.

For certain recipes after flaking arrange the meat in a mound between the claws on the plate or stuff inside the carapace.

Starters and Salads

Oysters

My favourite memory of oysters is from a market called Halle de Lyon in France. The renowned French chef, Jean Vittard, had taken me there to have a breakfast of fresh oysters dipped in vinegar and enjoyed with a glass of Chablis. The oysters still smelled of the sea; it was bliss. For me, eaten simply like this, with the minimum of fuss, is the best way to enjoy oysters.

But, having said that, there are a variety of ways to serve them to add a bit more flavour, colour and drama. Of the following, the Pizzaiola and Florentine are Italian inspired while the Garlic-Herb Cheese and the Black Olive Tapenade are reminiscent of France.

Oysters with Black Olive Tapenade

INGREDIENTS SERVES 4

24 fresh oysters

125 g (4 oz) black olives, pitted

1¹/₂ teaspoons minced garlic

2 tablespoons mashed
   anchovy fillets

1 tablespoon capers

¹/₄ teaspoon cayenne pepper

4 tablespoons olive oil

3 tablespoons grated Parmesan
   cheese

Shuck the oysters, leave on the half shell and arrange on a baking tray.

Place the olives, garlic, anchovy, capers and cayenne pepper in a food processor and pulse until the olives are broken down but the mixture remains chunky. With the machine running, add the oil in a slow steady stream and process until the mixture is finely chopped but not completely puréed.

Spread the mixture over the oysters, top with the cheese and bake in a pre-heated oven at Gas mark 4 (180°C/350°F) until the cheese melts. Serve immediately.

Oysters with Garlic-Herb Cheese

INGREDIENTS SERVES 4

24 fresh oysters

60 ml (2 fl oz) double cream

60 g (2 oz) cream cheese

1 tablespoon minced garlic

2 teaspoons freshly chopped basil

salt and pepper to taste

60 g (2 oz) grated Mozzarella cheese

60 g (2 oz) grated Gruyere cheese

Shuck the oysters and leave on the half shell.

Combine the cream and cream cheese in a bowl, then add the garlic, basil, salt and pepper. Whisk until the mixture is smooth, then spread over the oysters and sprinkle a mixture of the Mozzarella and Gruyere on top.

Place the oysters under a hot grill until the cheese melts and the tops are golden, then transfer to a platter and serve immediately.

Baked Oysters Pizzaiola

INGREDIENTS **SERVES 4**

24 fresh oysters

4 tablespoons olive oil

50 g (2 oz) chopped onion

25 g (1 oz) chopped garlic

1 teaspoon freshly chopped basil

$1/4$ teaspoon dried oregano

2 bay leaves

1 tablespoon mashed anchovy fillets

125 g (4 oz) plum tomatoes,
   skinned, seeded and diced

1 tablespoon chopped capers

50 g (2 oz) black olives, pitted
   and chopped

salt and pepper to taste

3 tablespoons grated Mozzarella
   cheese

3 tablespoons grated Gruyere
   cheese

Shuck the oysters, leave on the half shell and arrange on a baking tray.

Heat the oil in a saucepan, add the onion, garlic, basil, oregano and bay leaves and sauté for 2 minutes, then add the anchovy, tomato, capers and olives. Bring to the boil and simmer for 30 minutes, then remove the bay leaves and season with salt and pepper.

Allow to cool, then spread over the oysters and top with a mixture of the Mozzarella and Gruyere cheese. Pre-heat an oven to Gas Mark 4 (180°C/350°F) and bake the oysters until the cheese melts.

Oysters Florentine

INGREDIENTS **SERVES 4**

24 fresh oysters

125 g (4 oz) spinach

60 g (2 oz) butter

1 tablespoon plain flour

2 tablespoons finely chopped shallot

2 tablespoons dry white wine

250 ml (8 fl oz) fish stock

2 bay leaves

2 tablespoons single cream

salt and pepper to taste

75 g (3 oz) grated Emmenthal
   cheese

75 g (3 oz) grated Gruyere cheese

dash of cayenne pepper

Shuck the oysters, leave on the half shell and arrange on a baking tray. Blanch the spinach and chop finely. Make a roux with 1 tablespoon of butter and the flour.

Melt the remaining butter in a pan and sauté the shallot for 2-3 minutes, then add the wine, stock and bay leaves and bring to the boil. Add the cream and reduce liquid by half, then add the roux, a little at a time, to thicken the sauce. Remove the bay leaves, mix in the spinach and season with salt and pepper.

Spread the mixture over the oysters, top with the combined Emmenthal and Gruyere and add a dash of cayenne pepper, then bake in a pre-heated oven at Gas Mark 4 (180°C/350°F) until the cheese melts. Serve immediately.

Clam Stew

1 kilo (2^1/$_4$ lbs) clams

100 g (4 oz) roughly diced bacon

1 tablespoon minced garlic

100 g (4 oz) diced onion

200 g (7 oz) tomatoes, skinned,
  seeded and diced

60 g (2 oz) diced celery

2 bay leaves

75 ml (3 fl oz) dry white wine

2 teaspoons freshly chopped basil

salt and pepper to taste

This stew is lighter and simpler than the traditional chowder as it contains no cream but the bacon gives it a wonderful rich and smoky flavour. For a more substantial meal increase the quantities and serve with rice or noodles.

Wash the clams thoroughly in a bowl of water, then rinse under running water and drain.

Fry the bacon in a heavy-based pan to render the fat, then add the garlic, onion, tomato and celery and sauté for 4-5 minutes. Add the bay leaves, wine and 500 ml (18 fl oz) water and bring to the boil.

Simmer for 2 minutes, then add the clams and basil and bring back to the boil. Cook until the clams open, discarding any that fail to do so, then remove from the heat, season with salt and pepper and transfer to a serving bowl.

Mussel and Corn Salad

750 g (1 ^{1}/$_2$ lbs) mussels

2 tablespoons finely chopped onion

2 tablespoons finely chopped celery

2 teaspoons minced garlic

2 teaspoons dried fennel

1 teaspoon Pernod

2 tablespoons olive oil

1 tablespoon fresh lemon juice

salt and pepper to taste

100 g (4 oz) corn kernels

1 tablespoon diced red pepper

2 tablespoons diced celery

75 g (3 oz) young spinach leaves

Place the mussels in a bowl of fresh water and, using a small, hard brush, clean thoroughly, then rinse in cold water.

Place the onion, celery, garlic and fennel in a large saucepan, add 500 ml (18 fl oz) water and bring to the boil. Add the mussels and remove with a slotted spoon as they open, discarding any that fail to do so. Remove the mussels from their shells and allow to cool.

Strain the stock into a fresh pan and bring back to the boil to reduce the volume by half. Add the Pernod and simmer for a further minute, then remove pan from the heat and allow to cool.

Transfer 75 ml (3 fl oz) of the cooled stock to a mixing bowl, add the olive oil, lemon juice, salt and pepper and whisk to combine thoroughly.

Place the mussels in a bowl, add the corn, red pepper and celery and pour on the dressing. Toss lightly, then transfer to a platter lined with spinach leaves.

Baked Mussels Parmesan

1 kilo (2¼ lbs) mussels

125 ml (4 fl oz) white wine

300 g (10 oz) butter, softened

3 tablespoons chopped garlic

2 tablespoons chopped parsley

125 g (4 oz) Parmesan cheese

2 teaspoons paprika

rock salt

Place the mussels in a bowl of fresh water and, using a small, hard brush, clean thoroughly, then rinse in cold water, drain and place in a large saucepan.

Add the wine and bring to the boil. Cook for 3-4 minutes, shaking the pan frequently, then drain and discard any mussels that have failed to open. Discard the top shells and allow to cool.

Combine the softened butter with the garlic and parsley and spread over the mussels, then top with Parmesan cheese and a dash of paprika.

Arrange the half shells on a baking tray lined with rock salt. Preheat an oven to Gas Mark 4 (180°C/350°F) and bake for 3-4 minutes, then transfer to a platter also lined with rock salt and serve immediately.

Scallops Provencale

4 tablespoons olive oil

2 teaspoons minced garlic

75 g (3 oz) chopped shallot

150 g (5 oz) tomatoes, skinned, seeded and chopped

1 teaspoon freshly chopped thyme

1 tablespoon freshley chopped parsley

salt and pepper to taste

16 scallops on the half shell

3 tablespoons grated Parmesan cheese

3 tablespoons grated Gruyere cheese

rock salt

A cheese topping gives any shellfish a luxuriously creamy finish and this dish is further complemented by an aromatic herb medley.

Heat the oil in a saucepan and sauté the garlic and shallot until translucent, then add the tomato, thyme and parsley. Season with salt and pepper and simmer for 15 minutes.

Spoon a little sauce on to each scallop and top with a mixture of Parmesan and Gruyere cheese, then arrange the shells on a baking tray lined with rock salt.

Preheat an oven to Gas Mark 4 (180°C/350°F) and bake the scallops until the tops are golden, then transfer to a platter also lined with rock salt and serve immediately.

Clams, Mussels and Scallops see previous page

Shrimp and Sweet Potato Fritters

INGREDIENTS **SERVES 4**

250 g (8 oz) shrimps

300 g (10 oz) sweet potatoes,
  peeled & shredded

3 egg whites, lightly beaten

75 g (3 oz) cornflour

salt and pepper to taste

vegetable oil for frying

75 ml (3 fl oz) malt or cider vinegar

2 teaspoons minced garlic

1 tablespoon finely sliced shallot

1 teaspoon dark soy sauce

Wash the shrimps in lightly salted water and pat dry, then place a bowl together with the sweet potato, egg whites and garlic. Mix the cornflour with a small quantity of cold water and add to the bowl, then season to taste and stir to combine.

Heat the oil in a shallow frying pan and drop in spoonfuls of the mixture, then press with a spatula to flatten. Fry until golden brown and crispy, then remove with a slotted spoon, drain on kitchen paper and transfer to a warm serving plate.

Mix together the vinegar, garlic, shallot and soy sauce and serve as a dipping sauce.

Prawns in Chilli Garlic Sauce

INGREDIENTS SERVES 4

400 g (14 oz) fresh prawns
salt and pepper
1 tablespoon fresh lime juice
1 teaspoon sweet paprika
75 ml (3 fl oz) olive oil
2 tablespoons thinly sliced garlic
1 tablespoon finely sliced red chilli

Often served as part of a Spanish tapas selection, this simple to prepare dish is a long standing favourite starter at the Via Mare.

Shell and de-vein the prawns and season with salt, pepper, lime juice and paprika. Set aside for 15 minutes.

Heat the oil and sauté the garlic for 2-3 minutes, then add the prawns and chilli and toss for 1-2 minutes. Transfer to a warm dish and serve immediately.

Prawns in Chilli Onion Vinaigrette

INGREDIENTS SERVES 4

600 g (1¼ lbs) fresh prawns
450 ml (16 fl oz) vinegar
75 g (3 oz) diced red onion
2 teaspoons finely chopped red chilli
2 tablespoons olive oil
salt and black pepper to taste
1 tablespoon chopped spring onion

Shell and de-vein the prawns and marinate in half the vinegar for 30 minutes, then squeeze dry and place in a bowl.

Add the red onion, chilli, oil and remaining vinegar to the prawns and season with salt and pepper. Mix well and chill for 30 minutes, then transfer to a serving dish and garnish with the chopped spring onion.

Crispy Crab Fans

INGREDIENTS SERVES 4

12 egg roll wrappers
200 g (7 oz) crabmeat
2 tablespoons sultanas
75 g (3 oz) mung bean sprouts, chopped
2 teaspoons chopped spring onion
1 tablespoon mayonnaise
1 teaspoon cayenne pepper
salt and black pepper to taste
1 tablespoon plain flour
1 tablespoon warn water
oil for deep frying
2 tablespoons light soy sauce
2 tablespoons fresh lemon juice

Cut the egg roll wrappers into 10 cm (4 inch) circles and lay on a flat surface. Place the crabmeat, sultanas, bean sprouts, onion and mayonnaise in a bowl and mix well, then season with cayenne, salt and black pepper. Divide the mixture into 12 portions and place in the centre of the wrappers, then fold over, pinch the edges and seal with a mixture of flour and water.

Heat the oil until it starts to smoke, then lower heat and fry the crab fans until crispy and golden. Remove with a slotted spoon and drain on kitchen paper, then serve with a dipping sauce of soy sauce and lemon juice.

Gingered Jumping Prawns

INGREDIENTS **SERVES 4**

1 kilo (2$^1/_4$ lbs) live prawns

60 g (2 oz) fine strips of ginger

60 g (2 oz) fine strips of leek

30 g (1 oz) fine strips of red chilli

2 tablespoons sea salt

250 ml (9 fl oz) ginger ale

2 tablespoons light soy sauce

2 tablespoons sesame oil

2 teaspoons finely chopped
  green chilli

Wash the prawns in lightly salted water, rinse under running water, then pat dry.

Place the strips of ginger, leek and red chilli in a wok, add 500 ml (18 fl oz) of water and bring to the boil. Cook for 3 minutes, then add the ginger ale and bring back to a rolling boil. Add the prawns and cook for 2 minutes, then strain and transfer to a serving dish.

Combine 75 ml (3 fl oz) of the cooking liquid with the soy sauce and sesame oil, then stir in the finely chopped chilli and serve as a dipping sauce.

Stuffed Bittergourds

INGREDIENTS **SERVES 4**

3 bittergourds at 200 g (7 oz) each

FILLING

2 tablespoons diced shrimp

2 tablespoons diced tuna

1$^1/_2$ tablespoons diced oyster

2 tablespoons diced pork fat

1$^1/_2$ tablespoons diced water
  chestnut

1$^1/_2$ tablespoons diced button
  mushroom

1$^1/_2$ tablespoons diced shitake
  mushroom

2 tablespoons light soy sauce

2 tablespoons Chinese rice wine

1 tablespoon sesame oil

freshly ground pepper to taste

1 tablespoon cornflour

Crab and Shrimp Dumplings

*These Chinese-inspired dumplings have
a dough that becomes transparent when cooked.
If you have a busy schedule buy ready-made
wonton wrappers, which are readily available
in Asian food stores.*

Combine the ingredients for the filling in a bowl, then cover
and chill for at least 30 minutes.

To make the dough, sift the wheat starch, tapioca flour and
salt into a bowl, add 200 ml (7 fl oz) lukewarm water and mix
well, then cover and allow to rest for 10 minutes.

Roll the dough into a 25 mm (1 inch) cylinder, then cut into
15 mm ($1/2$ inch) lengths.

Flatten with a small rolling pin and spoon a portion of filling into
the centre of each piece, then fold up and crimp the top to secure.
Place in a steamer and cook for 3 minutes, then transfer to a
serving platter.

For the dipping sauce, combine the soy sauce, vinegar, sesame
oil and sugar and stir until the sugar is completely dissolved.

Cut off the ends of the gourds and, with the blade
of a slim knife, carefully remove all the seeds. Blanch
for 3 minutes in a pan of lightly salted boiling
water, then refresh in iced water and pat dry.

Combine the filling ingredients in a bowl, then cover and set
aside for 10 minutes before stuffing into the gourds. Place the
gourds in a steamer and cook for 12-15 minutes, then allow to
cool slightly before cutting into serving size pieces. Transfer
to a serving platter and coat with the sauce.

To make the sauce, heat the oil in a small pan and sauté the
ginger and garlic for 2-3 minutes, then add the oyster sauce, soy
sauce and stock and bring to the boil. Lower heat and simmer
for 3 minutes, then add the cornflour and stir until the sauce
is slightly thickened.

Crab and Shrimp Dumplings and Stuffed Bittergourds see previous page

Spicy Shrimp Burritos

300 g (10 oz) fresh shrimps

3 tablespoons fresh lime juice

sea salt to taste

freshly ground black pepper

1 teaspoon sweet paprika

75 ml (3 fl oz) olive oil

2 tablespoons chopped garlic

2 tablespoons chopped red chilli

125 g (4 fl oz) cider vinegar

1 tablespoon sugar

$1/2$ teaspoon cumin seeds

1 bay leaf

1 tablespoon finely chopped onion

4 tablespoons finely chopped green
   and red peppers

4 flour tortillas

1 avocado, pitted, peeled, finely sliced

1 tablespoon chopped coriander

Shell and de-vein the shrimps and rinse in lime juice, then drain and season with salt, pepper and paprika. Heat the oil in a pan and sauté half the garlic for 2-3 minutes. Add the shrimps and half the chilli and cook over a high heat until the shrimps are bright pink.

Pour the vinegar into a saucepan, add the sugar, cumin, bay leaf and remaining garlic and chilli and bring to the boil. Add the onion and the red and green peppers and allow to simmer for 5-6 minutes, then remove pan from heat and transfer to individual dipping bowls.

Grill the tortillas for 10-15 seconds on each side, then lay on lightly-oiled surface.

Place shrimps along the centre of each tortilla and top with avocado and coriander, then roll up and transfer to a warm platter and serve with the pepper relish dip.

Crab Salad Crepes

200 g (7 oz) crabmeat

50 g (2 oz) carrot julienne

50 g l(2 oz) leek julienne

50 g (2 oz) red pepper julienne

50 g (2 oz) cucumber, peeled, seeded
   and shredded

3 tablespoons mayonnaise

salt and pepper to taste

4 lettuce leaves

75 g (3 oz) plain flour

2 tablespoons cornflour

generous pinch of salt

1 egg plus 1 egg white, lightly beaten

2 tablespoons vegetable oil

1 tablespoon chopped coriander

Combine the crabmeat, vegetables and mayonnaise and season with salt and pepper, then cover and place in the refrigerator for 30 minutes.

To make the crepes, sift flour and the salt into a bowl. Add the eggs, oil and 225 ml of water and whisk until the batter is smooth, then stir in the coriander.

Place a 15 cm (6 inch) frying pan over a very low heat and add a portion of batter. Tilt the pan so that the batter evenly covers the flat surface and cook until set. Cook the remaining batter in the same manner and stack the crepes to cool.

To serve, place a crepe over the top of a ramekin dish, add a lettuce leaf and a portion of the crab salad. Allow the crepe to settle into the ramekin, then gather the edges to form a pouch and secure with a shred of spring onion. Alternatively, place a lettuce leaf over the crepe and roll into a cone, then fill with crab salad.

Smoked Salmon with Fennel and Cheese Flan

INGREDIENTS **SERVES 4**

175 g (6 oz) short crust pastry

2 tablespoons butter

150 g (5 oz) fennel bulb, thinly sliced

25 g (1 oz) thinly sliced leek

2 tablespoons dry white wine

3 tablespoons cottage cheese

3 tablespoons cream cheese

3 tablespoons double cream

4 tablespoons milk

1 egg, lightly beaten

1 teaspoon freshly chopped
   rosemary

salt and freshly ground white
   pepper

dash of cayenne pepper

75 g (3 oz) smoked salmon slices
   cut into thin strips

Line a 22 mm (9 inch) flan dish with the pastry and bake blind.

Heat the butter in a pan and sauté the fennel and leek until soft, then add the wine and reduce. Remove pan from the heat and allow to cool.

Place the two cheeses, cream, milk, egg and rosemary in a bowl and combine well. Stir in the fennel and leek and season with salt, pepper and cayenne, then pour into the pastry shell.

Preheat an oven to Gas Mark 4 (180°C/350°F) and bake the flan for approximately 15 minutes until the mixture is almost set. Add the strips of smoked salmon and bake for a further 10 minutes until the top is golden. Serve hot or cold.

Smoked Salmon Roulade

INGREDIENTS **SERVES 4**

200 g (7 oz) potato, boiled and
   mashed

4 tablespoons fresh
   mayonnaise

salt and pepper to taste

50 g (2 oz) fine strips of carrot

30 g (1 oz) shredded iceberg
   lettuce

30 g (1 oz) fine strips of celery

30 g (1 oz) fine strips of fennel

200 g (7 oz) smoked salmon fillet,
   thinly sliced

100 g (4 oz) assorted salad
   greens

A delicious and colourful way of serving smoked salmon. Makes a wonderful party snack or part of an hors d'oeuvre platter.

Place the mashed potato in a bowl, add the mayonnaise, salt and pepper and mix well. In a separate bowl, combine the carrot, lettuce, celery and fennel.

Line a flat board with cling film and lay the salmon on top. Spread a thin layer of potato over the salmon, then add a layer of the mixed vegetables. Roll up tightly and chill for at least 30 minutes.

To serve, cut the roll into 4 pieces and remove the cling film. Arrange on a serving platter and garnish with assorted salad greens.

Smoked Salmon and Capellini Timbale

INGREDIENTS **SERVES 4**

200 g (7 oz) thinly sliced
  smoked salmon
1 tablespoon olive oil
325 g (11 oz) capellini pasta
2 tablespoons capers, fried
  and drained

SAUCE

2 tablespoons olive oil
2 tablespoons finely chopped onion
75 g (3 oz) smoked salmon trimmings
2 tablespoons chopped dill
125 ml (4 fl oz) dry white wine
450 ml (15 fl oz) fish stock
350 ml (12 fl oz) double cream
salt and pepper to taste

Bring a pan of water to the boil and add the oil and capellini. Cook at a rolling boil for approximately 2 minutes, until just tender, then rinse under cold water, drain and set aside.

Line a 1 litre (2 pint) mould with cling film and line the bottom and sides with three quarters of the salmon slices. Fill up with the pasta and top with the remaining salmon, folding the edges in to fully enclose the pasta, then cover loosely with cling film and place in a steamer.

Cook over rapidly boiling water for 2–3 minutes making sure the pasta is heated through but the salmon is not overcooked, then transfer to a serving dish, top with the sauce and garnish with the fried capers.

To make the sauce, heat the oil in a saucepan, add the onion and cook over a low heat for 5 minutes. Add the salmon trimmings, dill, wine, stock and cream and bring to the boil. Lower heat and simmer gently for 25 minutes until the sauce has thickened, then season to taste with salt and pepper.

Crab and Mango Salad

INGREDIENTS **SERVES 4**

1.5 kilos (3 lbs) fresh crabs,
  to yield 200 g (7 oz) crab meat
1 teaspoon freshly chopped basil
2 tablespoons finely diced celery
2 tablespoons mayonnaise
1 tablespoon sour cream
salt and white pepper to taste
2 ripe mangoes
lettuce leaves

Steam the crabs and allow to cool. Crack the claws. Carefully extract the meat from the shell and place in a bowl, together with the basil, celery, mayonnaise and sour cream. Combine thoroughly and season with salt and pepper.

Cut each mango in half and discard the stone. With a small spoon carefully scoop out most of the flesh. Fill each half skin with the crab mixture and surround with the scallops of mango, then place on a bed of lettuce and garnish with crab claws.

Asian Caesar Salad with Crab Claws

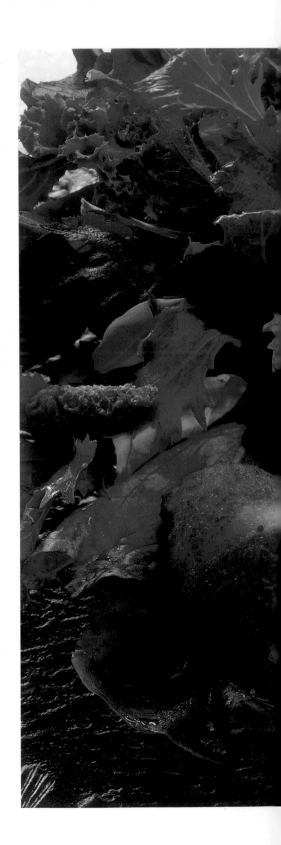

INGREDIENTS **SERVES 4**

60 g (2 oz) water chestnut flour

60 g (2 oz) plain flour

salt and cayenne pepper to taste

8 crab claws, steamed and shelled

1 egg, lightly beaten

vegetable oil for deep frying

300 g (10 oz) Chinese cabbage,
   or romaine lettuce, shredded

75 g assorted salad greens

DRESSING

2 egg yolks

1 teaspoon minced garlic

2 anchovy fillets, mashed

1 teaspoon Dijon mustard

$1/4$ teaspoon cumin seeds

$1/2$ teaspoon curry powder

1 tablespoon fresh lime juice

2 teaspoons finely chopped lime peel

75 ml (3 fl oz) extra virgin olive oil

125 g (4 oz) slivers Parmesan
   cheese

Combine the water chestnut flour, plain flour, salt and cayenne pepper in a bowl. Dip the crab claws in the beaten egg and coat with the flour mixture. Heat the oil until very hot and deep-fry the crab claws until golden and crispy, then drain on kitchen paper and set aside. Place the cabbage and salad greens in a bowl.

Place the egg yolks, garlic, anchovy, mustard, cumin seeds, curry powder, lime juice and rind in a small bowl and whisk to combine thoroughly. Add the oil in a slow steam and continue to whisk until the dressing emulsifies, then pour over the salad greens and toss lightly.

Transfer the salad to four dinner plates, top with slivers of Parmesan cheese and add 2 crab claws to each plate.

Fresh Anchovy Ceviche

INGREDIENTS SERVES 4

450 g (1 lb) fresh anchovies

150 ml (5 fl oz) vinegar

200 g (7 oz) grated coconut

2 tablespoons grated fresh ginger

2 tablespoons finely diced red onion

1 teaspoon finely chopped green chilli

1 teaspoon salt

freshly ground black pepper

fine strips of red pepper for garnish

Fresh anchovies are extremely delicate to handle and as a result can be difficult to find. But if you are able to find them this dish makes the effort worthwhile. Here you have a feel of Japanese 'sashimi' with the fish being only partially 'cooked' in the vinegar.

Gently press the body of the anchovies between the fingertips to loosen the flesh from the bone, then butterfly and remove heads and spines. Wash under cold running water, then rinse in 3 tablespoons of vinegar.

Add the remaining vinegar to the grated coconut and mash well, then squeeze to extract the liquid and strain into a bowl. Add the ginger, onion, chilli and anchovies and season with salt and pepper.

Mix well and chill for 1 hour, then transfer to a serving platter and garnish with the strips of red pepper.

Fish Tempura and Lentil Salad

INGREDIENTS SERVES 4

400 g (14 oz) fillet of grouper,
  or any firm fleshed fish
salt and pepper
150 g (5 oz) plain flour
2 tablespoons cornflour
pinch bicarbonate of soda
1 egg yolk, lightly beaten with
  175 ml (6 fl oz) iced water
oil for deep frying
6 tablespoons dashi (see note right)
2 tablespoons mirin (rice wine)
2 tablespoons dark soy sauce
1 tablespoon sugar
2 tablespoons grated daikon radish
1 tablespoon grated ginger
2 teaspoons olive oil
3 tablespoons diced onion
75 g (3 oz) lentils, soaked overnight
75 g young spinach leaves

A taste of Japan with this recipe. The base for the dipping sauce is 'dashi' which is the basic Japanese soup stock made from dried fish (bonito) and seaweed. It is available in dried or liquid form from many shops stocking Asian ingredients. Mirin is a sweet sake used exclusively for cooking. A sweet sherry could be used instead.

Slice the fish into serving size pieces, season with salt and pepper and dredge in a little plain flour. Sift the remaining flour, cornflour and baking powder into a bowl and add the beaten egg yolk. Stir to blend but take care not to over mix.

Heat the oil in a wok until it starts to smoke. Dip the fish into the batter, a few pieces at a time, then shake off excess and deep-fry until golden. Drain on a kitchen towel and keep warm.

Combine the dashi, mirin, soy sauce and sugar in a saucepan and place over a moderate heat until the sugar dissolves. Allow to cool, then add the radish and ginger and stir well.

Heat the olive oil and cook the onion until translucent, then drain the lentils and add to the pan. Add seasonings to taste and cover with water. Bring to the boil, then lower heat, cover the pan and simmer for 15 minutes. Remove pan from the heat and allow to cool, then strain and toss with 4 tablespoons of the mirin sauce.

To serve, line a plate with spinach leaves, arrange a mound of lentils in the centre and top with the pieces of fish.

Prawn Oriental Salad

INGREDIENTS SERVES 4

16 large prawns
salt and pepper
60 g (2 oz) butter
2 teaspoons light soy sauce
100 g (4 oz) green pepper, shredded
100 g (4 oz) red pepper, shredded
100 g (4 oz) onions, thinly sliced
200 g (7 oz) bean sprouts
150 g (5 oz) enoki mushrooms
200 g (7 oz) cantaloupe, shredded

Shell and de-vein the prawns, leaving the tails attached, then season with salt and pepper.

Melt the butter in a pan, add the soy sauce and sauté the prawns for 2 minutes, until pink, then remove and set aside. Add the peppers and onion to the pan and stir for 1 minute, then add the bean sprouts and toss for 30 seconds. Remove pan from heat and allow to cool.

To serve, arrange the vegetables, mushrooms and cantaloupe in a mound, top with the prawns and drizzle with a balsamic vinegar and oil dressing.

Swordfish and Vegetable Salad

INGREDIENTS SERVES 4

400 g (14 oz) swordfish fillet

100 g (4 oz) mayonnaise

2 teaspoons wasabi paste

125 ml (4 fl oz) apple juice

75 ml (3 fl oz) dark soy sauce

3 tablespoons sesame oil

salt and pepper to taste

125 g (4 oz) diced courgette

125 g (4 oz) diced shitake
   mushrooms

125 g (4 oz) diced potato

125 g (4 oz) diced carrot

1 tablespoon freshly chopped basil

salad greens for garnish

Cut the swordfish into 8 thin slices and place in a shallow dish. Combine the mayonnaise and wasabi paste and set aside.

Mix together the apple juice, soy sauce and sesame oil. Add 75 ml (3 fl oz) to the fish and place in the refrigerator for 2 hours. Then, remove fish from the marinade, season with salt and pepper and cook in a steamer for 2-3 minutes. Allow to cool.

Blanch the vegetables for 2 minutes, then strain, allow to cool and place in a bowl. Add the basil and 75 ml (3 fl oz) of the dressing and toss to combine.

To serve, place a slice of the fish in the centre of 4 salad plates, add a layer of vegetables, a dollop of wasabi mayonnaise and top with a further slice of fish. Drizzle with the remaining apple dressing and surround with teaspoons of the remaining mayonnaise. Garnish with mixed salad greens.

Herring and Beet Salad

200 g (7 oz) cooked beets

150 g (5 oz) herring fillets

1 teaspoon salt

$1/2$ teaspoon freshly ground
   black pepper

75 g (3 fl oz) malt vinegar

250 ml (9 fl oz) sour cream

2 teaspoons wasabi paste

1 teaspoon Dijon Mustard

2 teaspoons sugar

2 tablespoons balsamic vinegar

100 g (4 oz) shredded apple

75 g (3 oz) finely chopped onion

4 french beans

2 teaspoons finely chopped chives

12 quail eggs, marbled and shelled

Peel and slice the beets. Slice the herring diagonally into 15 mm (3/4 inch) strips and place in a shallow dish. Season with salt and pepper, add the malt vinegar and leave for 2 minutes, then strain and pat dry.

In a non-reactive bowl, whisk together the sour cream, wasabi, mustard, sugar and vinegar. Pour half of the mixture over the herring, cover and place in the refrigerator.

Combine the beet, apple and onion with the remaining cream mixture, cover and place in the refrigerator for at least 2 hours.

To serve, arrange the French beans in the centre of a platter and add a mound of the beet and apple mixture. Arrange the strips of herring on top, sprinkle with chopped chives and surround with the quail eggs.

To marble quail eggs, boil the eggs for 2 minutes, then rinse under cold water. With the back of a spoon, carefully make tiny cracks all over the shell. Place 2 teabags in a saucepan, add 350 ml water (12 fl oz) and bring to the boil. When the water turns dark add the quail eggs and lower heat to a bare simmer. Leave for 1 minute, then remove pan from heat and let the eggs cool in the liquid.

Mackerel in Coconut Vinaigrette

450 g (1 lb) mackerel fillets

225 ml (8 fl oz) vinegar

225 g (8 oz) grated coconut

6 shallots, thinly sliced

2 tablespoons chopped ginger

1 tablespoon finely chopped
   red chilli

2 teaspoons sea salt

$1/2$ teaspoon freshly ground
   black pepper

onion rings for garnish

Cut the fish into small cubes and rinse in half the vinegar. Combine the remaining vinegar and the coconut in a non-reactive bowl, then extract the juice and strain into a glass bowl.

Add the fish cubes, shallot, ginger and chilli, then season, cover and chill for at least 1 hour.

To serve, transfer to a platter and garnish with onion rings.

Seared Tuna with Cucumber Salad

INGREDIENTS SERVES 4

350 g (12 oz) loin of tuna

$^1/_2$ teaspoon salt

$^1/_4$ teaspoon freshly ground pepper

1 teaspoon sesame oil

2 tablespoons light soy sauce

2 tablespoons olive oil

75 ml (3 fl oz) fish stock

SALAD

200 g (7 oz) cucumber, seeded
  and thinly sliced

30 g (1 oz) shredded red pepper

1 teaspoon freshly chopped basil

1 teaspoon fresh lime juice

$^1/_2$ teaspoon rock salt

125 g (4 oz) mixed salad leaves

1 tablespoon toasted sesame
  seeds

Season the tuna with salt and pepper and place in a shallow dish. Combine the sesame oil, soy sauce, olive oil and fish stock and pour half over the tuna. Reserve the other half in the refrigerator. Cover the tuna and place in the refrigerator for 2 hours.

Heat a non-stick pan over a high heat and when the pan is very hot add the tuna and turn to sear on all sides, then remove the fish and allow to rest for 10 minutes before cutting into 1 cm ($^1/_2$ inch) sticks.

To make the salad, combine the cucumber, red pepper, basil, lime juice and rock salt and allow to stand for 15-20 minutes.

To serve, line one corner of a platter with the salad greens, add a mound of cucumber salad and surround with slices of tuna. Drizzle with reserved marinade and sprinkle the sesame seeds on top.

Lobster and Pomelo Salad

INGREDIENTS SERVES 4

2 lobster tails to yield 400 g
   (14 oz) meat
2 pomelos, peeled and segmented
200 g (7 oz) shredded daikon radish
100 ml (4 fl oz) olive oil
2 tablespoons vinegar
$1/2$ teaspoon mustard
$1/4$ teaspoon sugar
$1/2$ teaspoon sea salt
$1/2$ teaspoon freshly ground
   black pepper
lettuce leaves
150 g (5 oz) crispy fried noodles

*The pomelo is the largest of the citrus fruits
and is an 'ancestor' of the grapefruit. It has a thick
skin and a bitter pulp and is usually available at
Asian food markets.*

Carefully remove the meat from the lobster tails and cut into scallops, then place in a bowl. Set aside 8 pomelo segments for garnish. Flake the remainder and combine with the shredded radish.

Pour the olive oil and vinegar into a bowl, add the mustard, sugar, salt and pepper and combine with a wire whisk, then add 2 tablespoons to the lobster and toss lightly.

Line a salad plate with lettuce leaves, arrange the noodles in the centre and top with the pomelo-radish mixture. Surround with the lobster scallops and pomelo wedges and drizzle generously with the remaining vinaigrette.

Summer Seafood Salad

INGREDIENTS SERVES 4

750 g ($1^1/2$ lbs) mussels
2 onion rings
2 cloves smoked garlic
sprig of parsley
150 g (5 oz) fresh prawns
150 g (5 oz) squid, sliced into rings
3 tablespoons fresh lime juice
125 ml (4 fl oz) olive oil
1 tablespoon fish sauce
2 tablespoons honey
75 g (3 oz) diced pineapple
1 kiwi fruit, diced
75 g (3 oz) diced cucumber
salt and pepper to taste
75 g (3 oz) assorted salad greens
1 orange, segmented
fresh basil leaves for garnish

*An aptly named salad with a cool mix of seafood
and fruits and with a dressing that offers a
mixture of sweet, sour and salty tastes.*

Place the mussels in a bowl of fresh water and, using a small, hard brush, clean thoroughly, then rinse in cold water and drain.

Place the onion rings, garlic and parsley in a pot of water and bring to the boil. Add the mussels and, as each one opens, remove with a slotted spoon. Discard those that fail to open. Poach the prawns in the same stock until they turn pink, then remove and, once cool, shell and de-vein.

Bring the stock back to the boil and poach the squid rings for 2-3 minutes, then remove and allow to cool. Place the seafood in a bowl, cover and chill for at least 30 minutes.

Just prior to serving, whisk together the lime juice, oil, fish sauce and honey, then add the seafood, diced fruit and cucumber. Season to taste and toss lightly, then transfer to a serving platter, surround with the orange segments and garnish with basil leaves.

Summer Seafood Salad see previous page

Soups

Seafood in Sour Broth

INGREDIENTS SERVES 4

300 g (10 oz) mussels and clams

200 g (7 oz) fresh prawns

150 g (5 oz) green tamarind

1 litre (1½ pints) rice wash

100 g (4 oz) onions, diced

200 g (7 oz) tomatoes, skinned,
  seeded and diced

100 g (4 oz) banana heart, shredded

60 g (2 oz) daikon radish, sliced

60 g (2 oz) green beans, sliced

60 g (2 oz) aubergine, sliced

4 green chillies

60 g (2 oz) water cabbage,
  or spinach

100 g (4 oz) scallops, shelled

100 g (4 oz) milkfish bellies,
  cut into chunks

1 teaspoon fish sauce

The sourness of this soup comes from the tamarind which also enhances the flavour of both the seafood and the vegetables. Rice wash is the liquid left after adding water to rice and then rubbing the rice between your fingers. The resultant liquid is customarily used in Asia for sour soups.

Scrub and rinse the mussels and clams. Shell the prawns, leaving the tails intact.

Boil the tamarind with 250 ml (9 fl oz) of water until tender, then mash and pass through a strainer. Reserve the juice and discard the pulp.

Pour the rice wash into a saucepan, add the onion and tamarind juice and bring to the boil. Add the tomato, banana heart, radish and string beans and simmer for a further 10 minutes. Add the prawns, aubergine, chillies and cabbage and simmer for 2 minutes, then add the remaining seafood.

Continue cooking until the clams and mussels are open, discarding any that fail to do so, then season with fish sauce, transfer to a soup tureen and serve immediately.

Lobster Soup with Lime

INGREDIENTS SERVES 4

2 medium size lobsters

1.5 litres (2 ½ pints) fish stock

3 cloves garlic, crushed

2 tablespoons fish sauce

½ tablespoon sugar

2 teaspoons salt

2 spring onions, finely sliced

1 teaspoon finely sliced red chilli

2 tablespoons fresh lime juice

4 fresh basil leaves

Pour the fish stock into a saucepan, add the garlic and bring to the boil. Add the fish sauce, sugar and salt and boil for 1 minute. Add the lobsters and cook over a moderate heat until the lobsters are bright red, then remove pan from the heat. Remove the meat from the lobsters, cut into bite size chunks and place in individual soup bowls. If the lobsters are female, release the pinkish orange coral from the head and add to the bowls.

Strain the stock into a fresh pan and bring back to the boil. Add the spring onion and chilli and simmer for 1 minute, then pour over the lobster. Sprinkle with lime juice, garnish with basil leaves and serve immediately.

Crab Bisque with Pan-Fried Mullet

INGREDIENTS **SERVES 4**

1 kilo (2 1/4 lb) fresh blue shell crabs

2 tablespoons olive oil

1 tablespoon minced garlic

100 g (4 oz) onion, diced

75 g (3 oz) leek, diced

75 g (3 oz) celery, diced

75 g (3 oz) carrots, sliced

2 bay leaves, crumbled

2 teaspoons black peppercorns

1 teaspoon paprika

125 ml (4 fl oz) brandy

1.2 litres (2 quarts) fish stock

250 ml (9 fl oz) double cream

salt and pepper to taste

3 tablespoons butter

8 fillets of red mullets,
   75 g (3 oz) each

2 tablespoons fresh lime juice

4 sprigs of fresh basil

Use blue shell crabs for this recipe as their shells are relatively soft and can be minced in a food processor without causing damage.

Clean the crabs and, with a sharp cleaver cut the crabs in half.

Heat the oil in a saucepan, add the garlic, onion, leek, celery, carrot and bay leaves and sauté until the vegetables are softened. Add the crab, peppercorns and paprika, then pour in the brandy and flambé. Pour in the stock and simmer for 20 minutes, then remove from the heat, strain into a fresh saucepan and allow to cool. Remove the crabmeat and set aside.

Smash the crab shell and place in a food processor. Add the softened vegetables and process on a medium speed, then add to the stock. Bring to the boil, then lower heat, and simmer until the liquid has reduced to 500 ml (18 fl oz). Stir in the cream and continue to simmer, whisking continuously, then season to taste with salt and pepper.

Meanwhile heat the butter, add the mullet fillets, sprinkle with lime juice and cook until lightly browned. Place two fillets in the centre of each soup bowl, add the crabmeat and ladle the broth over the top. Garnish each bowl with a sprig of fresh basil.

Oysters and Pearls in Pumpkin Cream

4 small pumpkins

3 tablespoons small tapioca pearls

rock salt

12 oysters

2 tablespoons butter

100 g (4 oz) onions, diced

1 tablespoon minced garlic

1 litre (1 ³/₄ pints) fish stock

250 ml (9 fl oz) double cream

salt and pepper to taste

Steam the pumpkins, then remove the tops and square the bases so the pumpkins, to be used as 'soup bowls', stand upright. Scrape out the flesh (this should yield approximately 200 g (7 oz) of flesh, but be sure to leave sufficient in the pumpkins to retain the soup).

Pour 1 litre (1³/₄ pints) of water into a saucepan and bring to the boil. Add the tapioca pearls, reduce the heat and simmer, stirring occasionally and adding chilled water if necessary, until the tapioca is translucent (approximatey 25 minutes), then rinse under running water and drain.

Line a baking tray with rock salt and top with the oysters. Bake in a pre-heated oven at Gas Mark 4 (180°C/350°F) for about 5 minutes. As soon as the oysters open remove from the oven.
While still hot, drain the juice from the oysters into a bowl, add the tapioca and allow to marinate for 1 hour. Remove oysters from their shells and keep warm.

Heat the butter in a pan and fry the garlic and onion until translucent, then add the pumpkin flesh and the stock and bring to the boil. Reduce the heat and simmer for 4-5 minutes, then pour into a blender and purée until smooth.

Pour the soup back into the pan and bring back to the boil, then add the tapioca together with the marinade. Stir well, then ladle into the pumpkins and top with oysters. Serve immediately.

Portuguese Seafood Chowder

INGREDIENTS SERVES 4

250 g (8 oz) mussels

1 litre (1³/₄ pints) fish stock

2 tablespoons vinegar

2 teaspoons salt

150 g (5 oz) cod fillet

100 g (4 oz) diced bacon

1 tablespoon minced garlic

125 g (4 oz) diced onion

2 potatoes, peeled and diced

pinch of saffron

salt and pepper to taste

1 tablespoon chopped parsley

In this version of the classic New England dish the potatoes are coarsely mashed and the soup is coloured with saffron.

Place the mussels in a bowl of water and scrub with a small hard brush, then rinse in cold water.

Boil 250 ml (8 fl oz) of fish stock with the vinegar and half the salt. Plunge the mussels into the stock and, as they open, remove them with a slotted spoon. Discard any that fail to open. In the same stock poach the cod until barely cooked, then strain and add to the remaining stock. Flake the cod, remove the mussels from their shells and place in a bowl. Moisten with a little stock, cover and set aside.

Over a low heat fry the bacon to render the fat, then add the garlic and onion and sauté for 3 minutes. Pour in the stock and bring to the boil, then add the potato and saffron and simmer until the potato is tender.

With a slotted ladle, remove half of the diced potato, mash coarsely and return to the soup. Add the cod and mussels and season with salt and pepper. Bring back to the boil, then immediately pour into individual soup bowls and sprinkle with chopped parsley.

New England Clam Chowder

INGREDIENTS SERVES 4

300 g (10 oz) clams

2 tablespoons butter

125 (4 oz) butter

125 (4 oz) bacon, diced

125 g (4 oz) onion, diced

2 tablespoons plain flour

200 g (7 oz) potatoes, diced

1 teaspoon chopped fresh thyme

salt and freshly ground black pepper

500 ml (18 fl oz) milk

500 ml (18 fl oz) double cream

1 tablespoon chopped parsley

Scrub the clams and rinse in cold water. Place 600 ml (1 pint) of water in a pan, add the clams and cook until they open, discarding any that fail to do so. Allow to cool, then remove clams from the shells and chop coarsely. Strain and reserve half the broth.

Heat the butter and fry the bacon and onion until the onion is translucent. Add the flour and cook for a further 2 minutes. Pour in the reserved broth and bring to the boil. Add the potatoes, thyme and pepper and cook until the potatoes are tender.

Add the chopped clams and cook over a moderate heat for 8–10 minutes, then add the milk and cream and stir over a low heat, but do not allow to boil. Adjust seasonings to taste, then transfer to 4 individual soup bowls and sprinkle with chopped parsley.

Asian Fish Chowder

INGREDIENTS **SERVES 4**

500 g (1 lb 2 oz) fish head and bones

1 medium onion, diced

2 tomatoes, quartered

2 stems lemon grass, bulbs bruised

4 fresh red chillis

4 large fresh prawns

200 g (7 oz) grouper fillet,
   or other firm white fish

200 g (7 oz) taro root, diced

3 tablespoons diced daikon radish

60 g (2 oz) string beans, cut into
   1 cm ($^1/_2$ inch) lengths

3 tablespoons aubergine, peeled
   and diced

60 g (2 oz) water cabbage or
   spinach, shredded

1 tablespoon tamarind powder

fish sauce to taste

Place 2 litres (3 $^1/_2$ pints) of water in a large pot, add the fish head and bones, the onion, tomato, lemon grass and chillies and bring to the boil. Boil for 5 minutes, then add the prawns and fish. Remove when the prawns turn red and the fish is barely cooked. Shell and de-vein the prawns, leaving the tails attached. Return the heads and shell to the stock and boil for a further 5 minutes, then strain into a fresh pan. Chop the prawns and flake the fish.

Reheat the stock, add the taro root and simmer until tender, then strain into a fresh pan. In a blender purée two-thirds of the taro with a little stock and set aside. Reserve the remaining taro for garnish. Bring the stock back to the boil and add the radish, beans and aubergine. Gradually add the tamarind powder, tasting for the desired degree of sourness, then allow to simmer for 3-4 minutes.

Add the puréed taro and water cabbage and cook for 1 minute, then add the prawns and fish and season to taste with the fish sauce. Cook for a further minute, transfer to a soup tureen and float the reserved diced taro on top. Serve immediately.

Sea Urchin and Cauliflower Cappuccino with Caviar

INGREDIENTS SERVES 4

2 tablespoons butter

1 teaspoon minced garlic

60 g (2 oz) finely sliced leek

1 medium tomato, peeled, seeded and chopped

60 g (2 oz) chopped cauliflower

750 ml (1¹/₄ pints) fish stock

250 ml (9 fl oz) crème fraiche

100 g (4 oz) sea urchin

2 teaspoons Pernod

salt and pepper to taste

juice of half a lemon

GARNISH

4 teaspoons crème fraiche

2 teaspoons Beluga caviar

Sea urchin is always a very special treat. Its creamy texture is just perfect for this soup and the topping of crème fraiche and caviar just triples the pleasure.

Heat the butter in a heavy pan and sauté the garlic, leek, tomato and cauliflower. Pour in the stock and simmer for 20 minutes. Fold in the crème fraiche, sea urchin and Pernod and simmer for a further 10 minutes, stirring continuously. Allow to cool slightly, then pour into a blender and puree until smooth. Season with salt, pepper and lemon juice.

Just prior to serving, reheat the soup and pour into the blender. Taking extra care because of the heat of the soup, blend at medium speed until the mixture becomes foamy. Pour into soup cups, then top with a teaspoon of crème fraiche and half a teaspoon of caviar.

Borscht of Dover Sole with Salmon Roe

INGREDIENTS SERVES 4

575 g (1¹/₄ lbs) whole Dover sole

3 tablespoons unsalted butter

60 g (2 oz) sliced onion

60 g (2 oz) sliced leek

1 tomato, quartered

¹/₂ teaspoon black peppercorns

1 baby carrot

60 g (2 oz) chopped celery stalks

60 g (2 oz) shredded cabbage leaves

2 boiled beets, sliced diagonally

2 tablespoons butter

salt and pepper to taste

1 tablespoon sour cream

2 teaspoons salmon roe

VEGETABLE TOPPING

30 g (1 oz) shredded leek

30 g (1 oz) shredded celery

30 g (1 oz) shredded carrot

1 orange, thinly sliced

Scale, clean and fillet the fish. Reserve the head, bones and trimmings for the stock. Skin and slice each fillet into serving pieces.

Heat the butter in a pan and gently sauté the onion, leek, tomato and peppercorns. Add the fish head and bones, pour in 2 litres (3¹/₂ pints) of water and bring to the boil. Simmer for 20 minutes, then strain the stock into a fresh pan and bring back to the boil. Add the carrot, celery and cabbage and cook for 2-3 minutes, then remove vegetables with a slotted spoon and place in individual soup plates. Add the beet to the stock and simmer for 2 minutes, then remove and transfer to the plates.

Meanwhile arrange the sole fillets on a sheet of buttered foil and season with the salt and pepper. Cover with the vegetable topping and moisten with a little of the soup stock, then fold up and seal the edges. Place the parcels in a preheated oven at Gas Mark 4 (180°C/350°F) and bake for 3-4 minutes, then open, discard the vegetables and place the fish in the plates.

Bring the stock back to the boil and strain into the soup plates, then add the sour cream and top with the salmon roe.

Clam Broth with Ginger and Lemon Grass

24 large clams

2 tablespoons olive oil

75 g (3 oz) spring onion, sliced

2 tablespoons shredded fresh ginger

2 lemon grass bulbs, crushed

1 tablespoon fish sauce

2 tablespoons shredded chilli leaves

Scrub the clams to clean and rinse in cold water.

Heat the oil in a pan and sauté the spring onion, ginger and lemon grass. Add 1.5 litres (2 $^1/_2$ pints) of water and bring to the boil, then add the clams and season with fish sauce. Remove any clams that fail to open, then add the chilli leaves to the broth. Stir for 30 seconds, then pour into a tureen and serve immediately.

Crystal Shrimp Dumplings in Noodle Soup

2 tablespoons diced shrimp

1 teaspoon diced pork fat

1 tablespoon sliced shitake mushrooms

2 teaspoons Chinese rice wine

$^1/_2$ teaspoon sugar

1 teaspoon cornflour

1 teaspoon chopped coriander leaves

1 tablespoon shredded carrot

salt and white pepper to taste

CRYSTAL DUMPLING DOUGH

125 g (4 oz) wheat starch

3 tablespoons tapioca flour

pinch of salt

BROTH

1.5 litres (2 $^1/_2$ pints) chicken stock

75 g (3 oz) sliced carrot

75 g (3 oz) water cabbage

1 tablespoon sliced oyster mushrooms

1 tablespoon sliced woodear mushrooms

75 g (3 oz) Chinese cabbage

2 tablespoons bean sprouts

125 g (4 oz) purple yam noodles or fresh egg noodles, blanched

2 teaspoons sesame oil

1 tablespoon chopped spring onion

If you are unable to buy water cabbage substitute watercress or young spinach leaves. Wheat starch and tapioca flour are available in Oriental shops, but if they are difficult to obtain use commercial wonton sheets instead.

Combine all the filling ingredients into a bowl, then cover and chill in the refrigerator.

Sift together the wheat starch, tapioca flour and salt in a bowl. Add 100 ml (4 fl oz) of lukewarm water and mix well. Cover and allow the dough to rest for 10 minutes, then roll into a 3 cm (1 inch) cylinder and cut into 2 cm ($^3/_4$ inch) wide slices. Roll each slice until smooth, flatten with a rolling pin and using a cutter make 5 cm (2 inch) discs. Place a teaspoon of the filling into the centre of each disc, moisten the edges with water and carefully fold to form a half moon. Press the edges to seal and steam for 3 minutes.

Bring the chicken stock to the boil, add the carrot, cabbage and mushrooms and simmer for 3 minutes. Add the Chinese cabbage and continue to simmer until wilted, then add the bean sprouts and sesame oil and adjust seasonings to taste. Strain the stock and bring back to the boil.

To serve, place the noodles, vegetables and dumplings into individual soup bowls, add the stock and garnish with the spring onion.

Main Course – Shell Fish

Pan-Seared Scallops with Broccoli

INGREDIENTS SERVES 4

600 g (1¹/₂ lb) scallops, out of shell

2 teaspoons lemon juice

salt and pepper to taste

2 tablespoons olive oil

1 teaspoon minced garlic

3 tablespoons diced onion

250 g (8 oz) tomatoes,
   skinned, seeded and finely diced

1 tablespoon shredded basil

2 tablespoons white wine

salt and pepper to taste

3 tablespoons clarified butter

SAUCE

2 tablespoons olive oil

¹/₂ tablespoon minced garlic

75 g (3 oz) chopped onion

300 g (10 oz) broccoli

125 ml (4 fl oz) chicken stock

2 tablespoons double cream

salt and pepper to taste

Season the scallops with salt, pepper and lemon juice and set aside.

Heat the oil and sauté the garlic, onion and tomatoes. Add the basil and white wine and simmer for 15–20 minutes, then season to taste and keep warm.

To make the broccoli sauce, heat the olive oil in a saucepan and sauté the garlic and onion for 3 minutes. Add the broccoli and continue to sauté for a further 2 minutes, then add the stock and bring to the boil. Stir in the cream and simmer for a further 5 minutes. Season to taste and purée in a blender.

Heat the butter in a pan and fry the scallops for 45 seconds on each side.

To serve, pour the broccoli sauce onto a warm platter and place a mound of the tomato mixture in the centre of the plate. Surround with the scallops and serve immediately.

Prawns with Potato Crust and Gazpacho Sauce

INGREDIENTS SERVES 4

16 king prawns

salt and pepper

300 g (10 oz) large potatoes,

60 g (2 oz) cornflour

oil for deep frying

1 tablespoon freshly
   chopped coriander

SAUCE

175 g (6 oz) tomatoes,
   coarsely chopped

2 tablespoons diced red pepper

3 tablespoons finely chopped onion

75 g (3 oz) cucumber,
   coarsely chopped

125 ml (4 fl oz) tomato juice

60 ml (2 fl oz) vinegar

60 ml (2 fl oz) olive oil

1 teaspoon freshly chopped basil

Tabasco sauce to taste

salt and pepper to taste

Shell and de-vein the prawns, leaving the tails attached, and season with salt and pepper.

Thread each prawn on to a very thin bamboo skewer to prevent it curling during cooking.

Peel the potatoes and shred very finely, so that the potato resembles vermicelli, and season with 1 teaspoon salt. Mix the cornflour with 2 tablespoons water and add to the potato. Combine well, then wrap a layer of potato around each prawn. Wrap the prawns tightly in cling film and place in the refrigerator for at least 1 hour.

When ready to serve, discard the cling film and deep fry the potato-encrusted prawns until golden and crispy, then remove, drain off excess oil and transfer to a platter. Pour the sauce alongside the prawns, garnish with freshly chopped coriander and serve immediately.

To make the sauce, purée the vegetables until smooth, then transfer to a bowl. Whisk together the tomato juice, vinegar and oil, then add to the vegetables, together with the basil, Tabasco, salt and pepper. Combine well, cover and chill for at least 30 minutes.

Prawns with Champagne Sauce

INGREDIENTS SERVES 4

450 g (1 lb) fresh prawns

2 teaspoons fresh lime juice

salt and pepper

1½ teaspoons olive oil

250 ml (9 fl oz) dry champagne

150 g (5 oz) unsalted butter, cubed

Shell and de-vein the prawns. Season with lime juice and season with salt and pepper. Brush the prawns with oil and cook on a hot griddle for 1-2 minutes until pink, then transfer to a warmed serving dish.

Pour the champagne into a small saucepan and bring to the boil. Simmer until reduced by half, then remove pan from the heat and whisk in the butter, one cube at a time. Adjust seasonings to taste, pour over the prawns and serve immediately.

ee prevoius page

Seafood with Roasted Coconut

INGREDIENTS SERVES 4

400 g (14 oz) fresh prawns

150 g (5 oz) fillet of sea bass

100 g (4 oz) squid, cleaned and prepared

8 scallops

200 g (7 oz) mussels

150 g (5 oz) clams

75 g (3 oz) young coconut flesh,
    cut into fine strips

2 tablespoons butter

2 tablespoons finely chopped onion

2 teaspoons minced garlic

2 teaspoons finely chopped ginger

2 tablespoons thinly sliced shitake
    mushrooms

3 tablespoons chopped red pepper

3 tablespoons chopped green pepper

2 teaspoons dark rum

175 ml (6 fl oz) fish stock

175 ml (6 fl oz) coconut cream

1/2 teaspoon chopped basil

salt and pepper to taste

large dash cayenne pepper

Shell and de-vein the prawns. Cut the sea bass and squid into bite-size pieces. Remove the scallops from the shell. Scrub and rinse the mussels and clams.

Spread the coconut strips on a baking tray and roast in a hot oven for 5 minutes.

Heat the butter and sauté the onion, garlic, ginger, mushrooms and peppers for 2-3 minutes. Pour in the rum, stock and coconut cream and bring to the boil. Lower heat, add the basil and simmer to reduce the sauce by half its volume, then season with the salt, pepper and cayenne.

Add the prawns, mussels, clams and sea bass and cook until barely done and most of the shells have opened, then add the scallops and stir for a further minute.

Transfer to a serving dish, discarding any mussels and clams that have failed to open. Top with the strips of roasted coconut and serve immediately.

Seafood Paella

INGREDIENTS SERVES 4

2 crab

150 g (5 oz) clams

200 g (7 oz) mussels

6 prawns

150 g (5 oz) squid

200 g (7 oz) snapper or grouper

2 tablespoons olive oil

100 g (4 oz) diced bacon

2 tablespoons minced garlic

3 tablespoons sliced onion

75 g (3 oz) sliced red and green
   pepper

100 g (4 oz) sliced spanish sausage
   such as chorizo

2 tablespoons paprika

1 teaspoon saffron

1 tin chopped tomatoes

2 bay leaves

500 g (1 lb 2 oz) long grain rice

1 litre (1 3/4 pints) chicken broth

75 g (3 oz) green beans

2 tablespoons peas

2 hardboiled eggs, quartered

12 black olives

2 lemons quartered

2 tablespoons chopped parsley

 Clean and prepare the crabs. Scrub the clams and mussels. Wash the prawns and trim the heads. Skin and score the squid and cut the fish into small batons.

Heat the oil in a paella pan and fry the bacon, then remove and set aside. Add the garlic, onion and peppers to the pan and sauté until translucent, then add the sausage and replace the bacon. Add the paprika, saffron, tomato and bay leaves and all the seafood and cook for 2 minutes.

Remove the seafood and set aside, then add the rice and broth and adjust seasonings to taste. Cook until the rice is barely tender, then add the beans and replace the seafood.

Cover tightly and cook for approximately 20 minutes until the broth has been completely absorbed by the rice, then add the peas.

Place the covered pan in a pre-heated oven at Gas Mark 4 (180°C/350°F) and bake for 20 minutes, then transfer to a large serving platter. Garnish with the eggs, olives, lemon and parsley and serve immediately.

Crab Claws in Chilli Sauce

INGREDIENTS SERVES 4

16 crab claws

2 eggs, lightly beaten

75 g (3 oz) water chestnut flour

75 g (3 oz) plain flour

vegetable oil for frying

2 tablespoons chopped onion

1 tablespoon chopped ginger

1 tablespoon chopped red
   and green chilli

2 teaspoons minced garlic

1 teaspoon chopped lemon
   grass bulb

125 ml (4 fl oz) tomato ketchup

1 teaspoon sesame oil

1/2 teaspoon salt

1/4 teaspoon black pepper

fresh coriander sprigs

Steam the crab claws, then allow to cool. Chill for 1 hour then remove shells.

Dip the claws in half the beaten egg, then dust with the combined flours. Heat the oil until it is very hot, then deep-fry the claws until golden and crispy. Remove and drain on kitchen paper and keep warm.

Heat 2 tablespoons of fresh oil in a saucepan and sauté the onion, ginger, chilli, garlic and lemon grass for 2–3 minutes, then add the ketchup, sesame oil and 125 ml (4 fl oz) of water and bring to the boil. Lower heat and allow to simmer for 5 minutes, then season with salt and pepper.

Whisk in the remaining egg, then add the crab and mix well. Transfer to a warm serving plate and garnish with sprigs of coriander.

Crabs in Roasted Coconut Sauce

INGREDIENTS SERVES 4

6 blue shell crabs
2 coconuts
2 tablespoons chopped onion
1 tablespoon ground turmeric
3 tablespoons chopped red chilli
3 tablespoons fish sauce
1 teaspoon freshly ground
   black pepper
6 whole green chillies

This recipe suggests making coconut cream and milk from the raw product but if this is not practical you can use tins of coconut cream and milk as can be purchased from supermarkets, although the roasted flavour will be missing.

Boil the crabs until bright pink, then smash into serving-size pieces.

Break open the coconuts and extract the flesh. Grate the flesh, spread on a tray and bake in the oven at Gas Mark 4 (180°C/350°F) until it starts to turn golden. Allow to cool, then wrap in cheesecloth and squeeze to extract at least 250 ml (9 fl oz) of coconut cream. Set aside.

Add 750 ml (1¼ pints) water to the remaining pulp and squeeze to extract lighter coconut milk. Place in a saucepan, add the onion, turmeric and chilli and bring to the boil. Reduce the heat and simmer for 3 minutes, then add the pieces of crab and season with fish sauce and pepper.

Simmer for a further 15 minutes, stir in the reserved coconut cream and add the whole chillies. Bring back to the boil and cook for a further minute, then transfer to a warm dish and serve immediately.

Crab with Garlic and Anchovy Sauce

INGREDIENTS SERVES 4

4 live crabs, 600 g (1¹/₄ lbs) each

salt and pepper

3 tablespoons olive oil

3 tablespoons minced garlic

2 anchovy fillets, mashed

450 ml (16 fl oz) fish stock

2 tablespoons fresh lime juice

1 teaspoon grated lime peel

2 tablespoons chopped fresh
 coriander

100 g (4 oz) butter

¹/₂ teaspoon ground black pepper

4 sprigs fresh coriander

Boil the crabs until bright pink, then break off the claws and set aside. Carefully remove all the meat from the crab shells, season with salt and pepper and place in the centre of a warm serving dish.

Heat the oil in a saucepan and sauté the garlic and anchovies for 2–3 minutes, then add the stock and bring to the boil. Continue to boil to reduce the stock by half, then add the lime juice and lime peel and cook for a further 2 minutes. Add the chopped coriander, butter and pepper and remove pan from the heat. Whisk vigorously until the sauce is smooth, then spoon over the crab.

Crack the claws and arrange around the sides of the plate, then garnish with sprigs of fresh coriander.

Stuffed Crab Shells Grilled in Banana Leaves

4 live crabs, 600 g (1¹/₄ lbs) each

2 tablespoons vegetable oil

2 tablespoons finely chopped onion

1 tablespoon finely chopped ginger

1 tablespoon minced garlic

1 tablespoon finely chopped
  red chilli

150 g (5 oz) freshly shredded
  young coconut

175 ml (6 fl oz) coconut cream

1 teaspoon fish sauce

¹/₂ teaspoon freshly ground
  black pepper

banana leaves for wrapping

Boil the crabs until bright pink, then allow to cool. Break off and crack the claws and carefully remove all the meat. Wash the shells and place in a warming oven.

Heat the oil in a pan and sauté the onion, ginger and garlic for 2-3 minutes. Add the chilli, coconut and coconut cream and bring to the boil, then immediately reduce heat and allow to simmer, stirring continuously, until the sauce thickens. Add the crabmeat, season with fish sauce and pepper and stir for 30 seconds, then transfer to the reserved shells.

Wrap the shells in individual banana leaves and tie securely, then place under a hot grill for 2-3 minutes, until the leaves are seared. Unwrap and serve immediately.

Crab in Turmeric and Lemon Grass Sauce

INGREDIENTS **SERVES 4**

1 kilo (2¼ lb) female soft shell crab

1 teaspoon minced ginger

125 g (4 oz) fresh coconut, shredded

75 ml (3 fl oz) coconut cream

2 teaspoons chopped spring onion

salt and pepper to taste

8 banana leaves, cut into 15 cm
  (5 inch) circles

750 ml (1¼pints) coconut milk

2 tablespoons sliced leek

2 stems lemon grass, bulb bruised

1 teaspoon ground turmeric

2 tablespoons chopped fresh ginger

2 tablespoons finely sliced red chilli

The original method of cooking this dish in the central provinces of the Philippines was to dig a hole on the beach, place charcoal embers in the hole and then lower a halved coconut containing crab and shrimp into the hole, letting the seafood cook in coconut milk. The following method may be less traditional but the results are just as tempting!

Clean the crabs and cut into quarters. Mix the crab fat with the ginger, coconut strips, 1 tablespoon of the coconut cream and half the spring onion. Season to taste, then divide into 8 portions and spoon on to the banana leaves. Fold up like a pouch and secure with a thin strip of banana leaf.

Place the pieces of crab in a heavy pan, add the coconut milk, leek, lemon grass, turmeric, ginger and chilli peppers and bring to the boil. Place a lid on the pan and simmer for 3-4 minutes, then add the banana leaf pouches and continue to simmer for a further 5 minutes.

Add the remaining coconut cream and bring back to the boil, then immediately remove from heat, transfer to a serving dish and sprinkle on the remaining spring onion.

Lobster with Goose Liver and Balsamic Reduction

INGREDIENTS SERVES 4

4 lobsters, 400 g (14 oz) each

200 g (7 oz) potatoes, coarsely grated

$1/2$ teaspoon salt

$1/4$ teaspoon pepper

4 tablespoons clarified butter

500 g (1 lb 2 oz) goose liver

2 tablespoons plain flour

250 ml (9 fl oz) balsamic vinegar

100 g (4 oz) unsalted butter, cut into small cubes

Boil the lobsters until bright red, then allow to cool. Remove the meat and cut into medallions.

Season the grated potato, divide into 4 portions and fry in half the clarified butter. Keep warm.

Cut the goose liver into 8 slices and sprinkle with flour. Heat the remaining butter in a pan and sear the liver slices for 30 seconds on each side, then drain on paper towels and keep warm.

Pour the balsamic vinegar into a pan and bring to the boil. Simmer until the volume is reduced to 75 ml (3 fl oz), then lower heat and whisk in the butter, a cube at a time.

To serve, place a potato pancake in the centre of 4 dinner plates and top with the lobster medallions and the goose liver. Drizzle the balsamic sauce around the side of the plates.

Lobster Hainanese

INGREDIENTS SERVES 4

4 lobsters, 500 g (1 lb each)

75 g (3 oz) thinly sliced ginger

75 g (3 oz) thinly sliced spring onions

1 teaspoon black peppercorns

2 tablespoons salt

500 g (1 lb 2 oz) long grain rice,
  soaked in cold water for 4 hours

3 tablespoons ghee, or clarified
  butter

1 tablespoon finely minced ginger

1 tablespoon minced garlic

1 tablespoon sesame oil

2 teaspoons salt

2 pandan leaves

75 g (3 oz) shredded cabbage

75 g (3 oz) thinly sliced cucumber

2 plum tomatoes, thinly sliced

GINGER CHILLI SAUCE

4 tablespoons peanut oil

2 tablespoons chopped ginger

2 teaspoons chopped green chilli

2 teaspoons salt

Pour 2 litres (3 ½ pints) of water into a large pan, add the ginger, spring onion, peppercorns and salt and bring to the boil. Add the lobsters (ensure they are covered by the water) and bring back to the boil. Reduce the heat and simmer for 15-20 minutes, skimming off the foam as it rises to the surface, then remove the lobsters, extract the meat and cut into medallions. Reserve the cooking liquid.

Drain the rice, rinse in cold water, then drain again Over a medium heat, sauté the ginger and garlic, being careful not to let it brown, then add the rice and sesame oil and sauté for a further couple of minutes. Add the pandan leaves, salt and 750 ml (1¼ pints) of the lobster broth and bring to the boil. Cook until almost all the broth is absorbed, then cover, reduce the heat and simmer for a further 10-12 minutes.

Pour the remaining lobster broth into a pan and bring to the boil. Add the cabbage until it begins to wilt, then pour into individual soup bowls.

To make the sauce, place all the ingredients in a blender and purée until smooth, then pour into a dipping saucer.

Arrange the cucumber and tomato slices on a large plate and top with the lobster medallions. Place the rice alongside and garnish with the sprigs of coriander. Serve with the bowls of broth and the dipping sauce.

Lobster Hainanese *see previous page*

Lobster with Spicy Coconut Crust

INGREDIENTS SERVES 4

4 lobsters, 450 g (1 lb) each

salt and pepper

2 teaspoons lime juice

150 g (5 oz) freshly grated coconut

75 g (3 oz) minced garlic

1 tablespoon chopped ginger

1 tablespoon diced red and green
   chilli pepper

1 tablespoon chopped turmeric

2 tablespoons lemon grass,
   bulb bruised

2 tablespoons chopped red onion

2 tablespoons fish sauce

juice and rind of 1 lime

175 ml (6 fl oz) coconut cream

1/4 teaspoon salt

1/2 teaspoon freshly ground pepper

Boil the lobsters until bright red, then butterfly each with a sharp chopper and discard the veins and waste sac. Season with salt, pepper and lime juice and leave to marinate for 15 minutes.

Roast the grated coconut until golden, allow to cool, then place in a blender together with all the remaining ingredients apart from the coconut cream and seasoning. Set the blender on low speed and gradually pour in the coconut cream to produce a smooth paste.

Coat the lobsters evenly with the paste and wrap individually in foil, then pre-heat an oven on Mark 4 (180°/350°F) and bake the lobster for approximately 30 minutes, until just cooked, then remove the foil and place under a hot grill until the tops are golden.

Cuttlefish Chinoise

INGREDIENTS SERVES 4

400 g (14 oz) cuttlefish

4 tablespoons oil

60 g (2 oz) chopped onion

30 g (1 oz) finely sliced ginger

2 teaspoons minced garlic

1 tomato, sliced into thin wedges

30 g (1 oz) sliced button mushrooms

30 g (1 oz) sliced leek

30 g (1 oz) finely sliced red pepper

1 tablespoon rice wine

2 tablespoons oyster sauce

1 tablespoon light soy sauce

salt and freshly ground black pepper

A quick stir- fry in a wok and a mixture of flavours from many sources (rice wine, oyster sauce and soy sauce) is all it takes to complete the culinary picture.

Pepare the cuttlefish, cutting the flesh into bite-size strips.

Heat 2 tablespoons of oil in a wok and sauté the onion, ginger, garlic, tomato, mushroom, leek and pepper for 2 minutes, then add the rice wine, oyster sauce, soy sauce, salt and pepper. Continue cooking until the vegetables are softened, adding a little water if necessary, then remove and set aside.

Wipe the wok, then add the remaining oil and bring to a high heat. Add the cuttlefish and stir-fry for approximately 1 minute, then replace the vegetables and cook for a further minute. Remove with a slotted spoon and drain off excess oil, then transfer to a dish and serve immediately.

Stuffed Squid

INGREDIENTS SERVES 4

700 g (1 lb 8 oz) small squid

salt and pepper

4 tablespoons olive oil

4 tablespoons chopped onion

2 tablespoons minced garlic

75 g (3 oz) carrot, diced

75 g (3 oz) tomato,
  skinned, seeded and chopped

4 tablespoons diced leek

150 g (5 oz) courgettes, diced

325 ml (12 fl oz) chicken stock

3 teaspoons tomato puree

2 tablespoons diced red pepper

2 teaspoons chopped fresh mint

175 g (6 oz) cooked couscous

Prepare and season the squid, reserving the tentacles.

In a saucepan heat the oil and sauté the onion until translucent. Add the garlic and carrot and cook for 2 minutes. Add the tomato, leek and courgette and continue to sauté for one minute, then pour in the stock and bring to the boil. Add the tomato puree and red pepper and simmer for a further 5 minutes. Stir in the mint and adjust seasonings to taste.

Combine half the mixture with the couscous and mix well, then stuff loosely into the squid, bearing in mind that the squid will shrink during cooking. Place the stuffed squid and the tentacles under a hot grill and cook for 1-2 minutes.

Place the remaining mixed vegetables on a serving dish and to top with the stuffed squid. Fill the openings of each squid with the tentacles and serve immediately.

Deep Fried Squid Tentacles with Sweet and Sour Sauce

INGREDIENTS SERVES 4

475g (1 lb) squid tentacles
salt and pepper
3 tablespoons minced garlic
1 egg, lightly beaten
300 g (10 oz) plain flour
oil for deep frying

SAUCE

2 tablespoons oil
1 tablespoon minced garlic
1 tablespoon chopped ginger
4 tablespoons chopped onion
1 teaspoon chopped red chilli
$^1/_2$ teaspoon chilli flakes
250 ml (8 fl oz) fish or chicken stock
2 tablespoons tomato ketchup
2 tablespoons oyster sauce
1 tablespoon sugar
$^1/_2$ teaspoon sesame oil
1 tablespoon cornflour, dissolved
   in 2 tablespoons water
salt and pepper

Cut the squid tentacles into bite-size pieces, place in a bowl and season with salt and pepper. Add the garlic, stir well and set aside for 30 minutes. Add the egg to the bowl and stir, then remove the squid and dredge in flour. Heat the oil until very hot, then deep-fry the squid in small batches until golden and crispy. Drain on kitchen paper, then transfer to a warm bowl, add the sauce and serve immediately.

To make the sauce, heat the oil and sauté the garlic, ginger, onion, pepper and chilli flakes. Add the stock, bring to the boil and simmer for 2 minutes. Blend until smooth, then return to the saucepan. Add the ketchup, oyster sauce, sugar and sesame oil and simmer for a further 2 minutes. Add the cornflour mixture and stir over a moderate heat for 3 minutes.

Squid *see previous page*

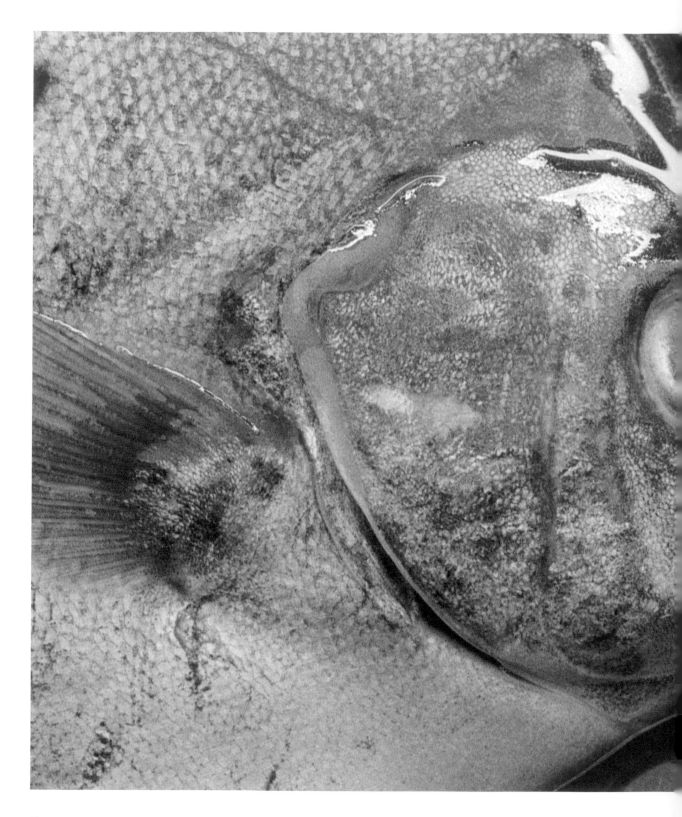

Main Course – Fish

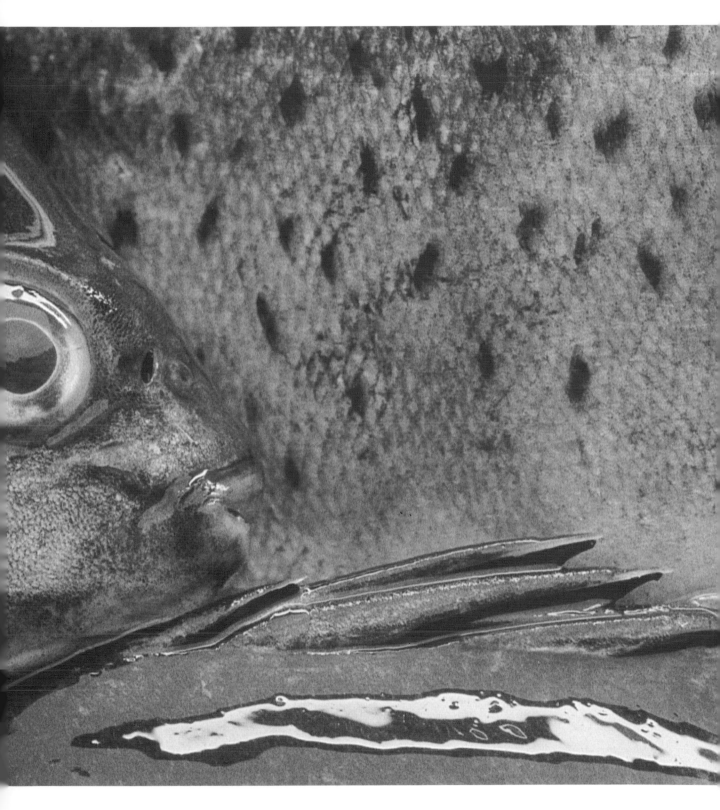

Halibut with Coulis of Spinach, Squash and Tomato

INGREDIENTS SERVES 4

4 halibut fillets, 200 g (7 oz) each
salt and pepper
2 teaspoons butter
175 g (6 oz) asparagus, blanched
and seasoned

SPINACH COULIS

2 tablespoons butter
2 tablespoons chopped shallot
1 tablespoon diced bacon
75 g (3 oz) spinach, blanched and
coarsely chopped
250 ml (9 fl oz) chicken stock

PUMPKIN COULIS

2 tablespoons butter
2 tablespoons chopped shallot
1 tablespoon diced bacon
100 g (4 oz) pumpkin, diced
250 ml (9 fl oz) chicken stock

TOMATO COULIS

2 tablespoons butter
1 teaspoon finely chopped garlic
3 tablespoons chopped onion
200 g (7 oz) tomatoes, skinned,
seeded and diced
250 ml (9 fl oz) chicken stock
1 tablespoon chopped fresh basil
salt and pepper

Remove half the skin from each fillet (see picture for finished result) and season with salt and pepper. Heat the butter in a non-stick pan and sauté the fish, first on the skin side for approximately 2 minutes, then for 1 minute on the other side.

For the spinach coulis, sauté the shallots in the butter until translucent then add the bacon and spinach and cook for a further 2 minutes. Add the stock and continue to cook for a further 2 minutes, then remove from the heat, blend until smooth and season with salt and pepper.

Follow the same procedure for the pumpkin coulis.

For the tomato coulis, melt the butter in a saucepan over a low heat and sauté the garlic and onion, until tender but not browned. Add the tomato and stock and simmer for 20 minutes, then add the basil and season to taste with salt and pepper. Remove pan from the heat and allow to cool slightly, then purée in a food processor.

To serve, reheat the coulis and spoon onto a plate in the shape of a triangle. Lay the asparagus on top and add the fish fillets.

INGREDIENTS SERVES 4

4 salmon fillets, 150 g (5 oz) each
salt and pepper
1 tablespoon lemon juice
3 tablespoons butter

SAUCE

2 tablespoons squid ink
2 tablespoons white wine vinegar
2 tablespoons olive oil
1 tablespoon minced garlic
60 g (2 oz) diced onion
1 medium tomato, diced
1 tablespoon chopped red chilli
1 bay leaf
75 ml (3 fl oz) clam juice
1 tablespoon butter
2 teaspoons plain flour
salt and pepper
30 g (1 oz) leek
30 g (1 oz) carrot
3 tablespoons plain flour
oil for frying

Salmon Fillet in Piquant Squid Ink Sauce

Season the salmon with salt, pepper and lemon juice. Heat butter in a frying pan and sear the salmon for 30 seconds on each side. Combine the squid ink and the vinegar, then strain and set aside.

Heat the oil in a pan over a medium heat and sauté the garlic, onion, tomato, chilli and bay leaf for 4-5 minutes. Add the clam juice and simmer for 10 minutes, then strain and set aside.

Melt the butter in a saucepan over a low heat and whisk in the flour. Add the combined squid ink and vinegar and whisk continuously, then season with salt and pepper.

Thinly slice the leek and carrot lengthwise and soak in iced water for 30 minutes, strain and wipe dry on kitchen towel, then dredge in flour and deep-fry until crispy.

Spoon some clam sauce into the centre of each plate, arrange the salmon fillets in the middle and top with the fried vegetables. Serve immediately with buttered pasta.

Salmon with Basil and Corn Salsa

INGREDIENTS SERVES 4

4 salmon steaks,
    175 g (6 oz) each
1 tablespoon lemon juice
salt and pepper
2 tablespoons chopped
    fresh basil
2 tablespoons chopped and
    roasted walnuts
2 teaspoons minced garlic
125 ml (4 fl oz) olive oil

CORN SALSA

100 g (4 oz) sweet corn kernels
75 g (3 oz) tomatoes, skinned
    seeded and diced
50 g (2 oz) cucumber, peeled
    seeded and diced
50 g (2 oz) red pepper
    seeded and diced
50 g (2 oz) green pepper
    seeded and diced
1 tablespoon chopped fresh
    coriander
4 tablespoons olive oil
salt and pepper

Marinate salmon steaks in lemon juice for 2 minutes, then season with salt and pepper and grill for 2 minutes on each side.

Place basil, walnuts and garlic in a blender and purée until smooth.

Combine all the corn salsa ingredients and mix well.

To serve, spoon warm basil sauce onto a plate, top with the salmon and place the salsa alongside.

Salmon *see previous page*

Rainbow Trout with Lobster Cream and Grapes

INGREDIENTS SERVES 4

4 trout, 350 g (12 oz) each

salt and pepper

50 g (2 oz) butter, softened

2 plum tomatoes, thinly sliced

100 g (4 oz) red onion, thinly sliced

4 sprigs fresh dill

4 teaspoons fish stock

250 g (9 oz) seedless grapes, peeled

1 tablespoon chopped parsley

SAUCE

2 tablespoons butter

50 g (2 oz) shallot , diced

50 g (2 oz) celery, diced

50 g (2 oz) carrot, diced

75 g (3 oz) tomato, diced

500 g (1 lb 2 oz) lobster head
  and shell, chopped

250 ml (9 fl oz) fish stock

4 tablespoons white wine

125 ml (4 fl oz) double cream

salt and pepper

Clean the fish thoroughly and season with salt and pepper.

Prepare 4 pieces of foil and spread with some of the butter. Lay each trout on a piece of buttered foil, top with the tomato slices, onion and a sprig of dill. Add a teaspoon of stock, dot with butter and seal the edges. Place on a baking tray and bake in a pre-heated oven at Gas Mark 4 (180°C/350°F) for 10 minutes.

To make the sauce, heat the butter in a saucepan and sauté the shallots, celery, carrots, tomato and lobster head and shell until they turn red. Add the stock and white wine and reduce the volume by half. Add the cream and simmer for about 20 minutes, stirring continuously. Strain and check seasoning.

To serve, transfer the fish to a serving dish and carefully remove the skin. Spoon the sauce around the fish and garnish with the seedless grapes and parsley.

Salmon with Spinach and Cheese Soufflé

INGREDIENTS SERVES 4

4 salmon fillets, 150 g (5 oz) each

1/2 teaspoon salt

1/4 teaspoon black pepper

1 tablespoon fresh lemon juice

2 tablespoons clarified butter

SOUFFLÉ

1 tablespoon plain flour

1 egg, separated

125 ml (4 fl oz) fresh milk

30 g (1 oz) spinach, blanched and
  squeezed dry

large pinch of nutmeg

Season the salmon fillets with salt, pepper and lemon juice and, in a non-stick pan, sear for 1 minute on each side. Spread an even layer of the soufflé on each fillet, add a sprinkling of Parmesan cheese and bake in a pre-heated oven at Gas Mark 4 (180°C/350°F) until the soufflé is puffed up and golden, approximately 7 minutes. Serve immediately.

To prepare the soufflé, place the flour, egg yolk and milk in a double boiler and cook until the mixture thickens. Add the mixture to the spinach, add the nutmeg and whisk to combine. Beat the egg whites until stiff. Stir a large spoonful of the egg white into the spinach, then gently fold into the remaining egg white.

Black Cod with Teriyaki Sauce

INGREDIENTS SERVES 4

4 fillets black cod, 200 g (7 oz) each
salt and white pepper
1 tablespoon fresh lime juice

TERIYAKI SAUCE

75 ml (3 fl oz) shoyu
   (Japanese soy sauce)
75 g (3 oz) sugar
1/2 tablespoon cornflour

Note that this dish has a richer flavour when the teriyaki sauce is slightly burnt, but it is important to half cook the fish before brushing with sauce to prevent the fish becoming charred.

Season the fish with salt, pepper and lime juice. Grill until half cooked, then brush with teriyaki sauce and continue cooking until done.

To make the sauce, place the soy sauce, sugar and 125 ml (4 fl oz) of water in a pan and bring to the boil, then reduce heat. Mix the cornflour with a little cold water and add to the sauce, then continue to simmer for 3 minutes.

Trout with Tomato and Pepper Salsa

INGREDIENTS SERVES 4

4 whole trout, 300 g (10 oz) each
salt and pepper
175 g (6 oz) yogurt
1 tablespoon freshly chopped basil
2 teaspoons minced garlic
dash of cayenne pepper
oil for shallow frying

SALSA

4 large plum tomatoes, skinned,
   seeded and sliced
50 g (2 oz) diced onion
50 g (2 oz) diced red pepper
50 g (2 oz) diced green pepper
50 g (2 oz) diced yellow pepper
1 tablespoon freshly chopped
   coriander
1 tablespoon minced garlic
1 tablespoon finely chopped red chilli
2 tablespoons fresh lime juice
salt and pepper

Remove the backbone from the trout and season with salt and pepper.

In a bowl, combine the yogurt, basil, garlic and cayenne pepper and stuff into the cavity of the fish. Cover in cling film and refrigerate for at least 1 hour.

Place all the salsa ingredients in a bowl, mix well and leave to stand at room temperature to allow the flavours to blend.

Heat the oil in a large frying pan and cook the trout over a moderate heat, turning once, until cooked and golden, then transfer to individual dinner plates and surround with salsa.

Sea Bass with Coconut Cream

INGREDIENTS **SERVES 4**

2 sea bass, 500 g (1 lb 2 oz) each
salt and pepper
1 tablespoon lime juice
2 tablespoons oil
2 banana leaves
2 teaspoons minced garlic
2 teaspoons chopped ginger
1 onion, chopped
2 tablespoons shrimp paste
1 teaspoon chopped red chilli
75 ml (3 fl oz) coconut milk
75 ml (3 fl oz) coconut cream
1 tablespoon chopped spring onion

Butterfly the fish, removing the backbone. Season the fish with salt, pepper and the lime juice. Brush with 1 tablespoon of the oil and wrap in a banana leaf. Grill till the fish is cooked.

Heat the remaining oil and sauté the garlic, ginger and onion. Add the shrimp paste, chilli and coconut milk and stir until the liquid is completely reduced. Remove from the heat, gently fold in the coconut cream and the spring onion.

To serve, unwrap the fish and transfer to a baking dish. Coat with the sauce and place under a grill until the top is golden brown.

Sea Bass with Chilli Beancurd Sauce

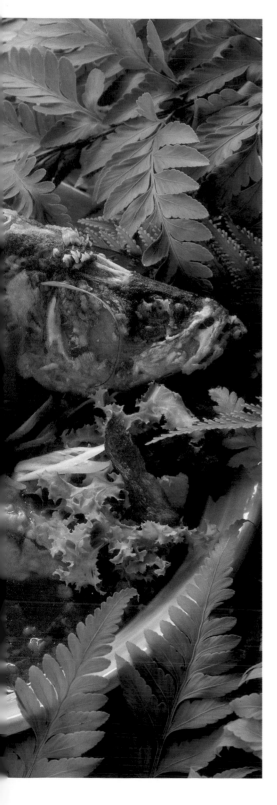

INGREDIENTS SERVES 4

4 whole sea bass, 350 g (12 oz) each

salt and pepper

125 g (4 oz) plain flour

125 g (4 oz) cornflour

oil for deep frying

25 g (1 oz) shredded lettuce

25 g (1 oz) shredded red chilli

25 g (1 oz) shredded spring onion

CHILLI BEANCURD SAUCE

2 tablespoons peanut oil

1 teaspoon minced garlic

1 teaspoon minced ginger

1 tablespoon chopped spring onion

1 tablespoon chopped red chilli

100 g (4 oz) minced pork

1 tablespoon dark soy sauce

3 tablespoons chilli sauce

2 teaspoons sesame oil

350 ml (12 fl oz) chicken stock

2 tablespoons salted black beans

200 g (7 oz) bean curd, diced

Scale and fillet the fish, taking care to keep the carcass intact. With a sharp knife carefully score the flesh of each fillet with criss-cross slits, then season with salt and pepper. Mix together the flour and cornflour and dredge the fillets. Heat the oil in a wok and fry the fish until the skin is golden and crispy, then remove and drain on kitchen paper. Arrange the fillets on a serving platter, pour over the sauce and garnish with the lettuce, chilli and spring onion.

To make the sauce, heat the oil in a pan and sauté the garlic, ginger, spring onion and chilli. Add the minced pork and continue to sauté until cooked, then add the soy sauce, chilli sauce, sesame oil and stock and simmer for a further 2 minutes. Rinse and blanch the salted black beans to reduce the saltiness and add to the sauce together with the beancurd. Adjust seasoning to taste.

Stuffed Milkfish

INGREDIENTS SERVES 4

500 g (1 lb 2 oz) whole milkfish

1 tablespoon lime juice

1 tablespoon light soy sauce

1/4 teaspoon freshly ground
black pepper

1 bay leaf

1 1/2 tablespoons finely chopped
celery

75 g (3 oz) onion

2 tablespoons vegetable oil

2 teaspoons minced garlic

100 g (4 oz) tomatoes, skinned,
seeded and chopped

75 g (3 oz) peas

75 g (3 oz) raisins

salt and pepper to taste

1 egg, lightly beaten

75 g (3 oz) grated Parmesan cheese

SAUCE

1 tablespoon olive oil

2 tablespoons finely chopped onion

1 teaspoon minced garlic

800 g (1 1/2 lb) tomatoes,
skinned, seeded and chopped

2 tablespoons cooked peas

salt and pepper to taste

With the side of a kitchen knife, gently pound the fish to loosen the meat from the skin, then break the big bone in the neck. Insert the handle of a tablespoon through the neck and carefully scrape the meat from the skin, pushing towards the tail. Break the bone at the tail end and pull out the bone and the meat. Set meat aside. Lay the skin in a shallow dish, add the lime juice, soy sauce and pepper and allow to marinate for 20 minutes.

Place the bay leaf, celery and half the onion in a saucepan. Add 450 ml (16 fl oz) water and bring to the boil. Reduce the heat and simmer for 5 minutes, then add the fish meat and simmer for a further 5 minutes. Strain and carefully remove any bones, then flake the meat and reserve the stock.

Heat the oil in a fresh saucepan and sauté the garlic. Add the tomato and the remaining onion and cook for 3 minutes. Add the peas, raisins, fish meat and season. Cook for a further 5 minutes. Allow to cool, then stir in the egg and cheese.

Stuff the mixture back inside the skin, brush with oil and place on a well-greased baking tray. Bake in a pre-heated oven at Gas Mark 4 (180°C/350°F) until the skin is golden, then transfer to a serving platter and top with the prepared sauce.

To make the sauce, heat the oil in a pan and sauté the onion, garlic and tomato for 3 minutes. Add 250 ml (9 fl oz) of the reserved stock and bring back to the boil. Simmer for 10 minutes, add the peas and season to taste.

Pompano with Egg Noodles and Vegetables

600 g (1lb) pompano (or sole) fillets
salt and pepper
125 (4 oz) plain flour
125 g (4 oz) cornflour
vegetable oil for deep frying
200 g (7 oz) fresh egg noodles
2 tablespoons peanut oil
30 g (1 oz) chopped onion
1 teaspoon finely chopped ginger
1 teaspoon minced garlic
30 g (1 oz) thinly sliced mushroom
30 g (1 oz) thinly sliced carrot
1 tablespoon chopped spring onion
1 tablespoon light soy sauce
1 teaspoon sugar
300 ml (10 fl oz) chicken stock
vegetable oil for deep frying

Cut the fish fillets into large slices, season with salt and pepper and dredge in a mixture of the plain flour and cornflour. Set aside.

Boil the noodles in a pan of boiling salted water for 2 minutes, then drain and set aside.

Heat the peanut oil in a pan and sauté the onion, ginger and garlic until softened, then add the mushroom, carrot and spring onion and continue to stir for a further 5 minutes.

Add the soy sauce, sugar and stock and cook for 1 minute, then thicken with a little cornflour and add the noodles. Combine well and transfer to a serving platter.

Heat the vegetable oil until it starts to smoke, then lower heat slightly and deep-fry the fish fillets until golden and crispy. Arrange the fillets over the noodles and serve immediately.

Deep Fried Pompano with Tomato Salsa

INGREDIENTS **SERVES 4**

450 g (1 lb) pompano (or sole) fillets

1 tablespoon fresh calamansi juice

1 teaspoon salt

1/4 teaspoon freshly ground
   black pepper

125 g (4 oz) plain flour

oil for deep frying

SALSA

6 tomatoes, skinned, seeded
   and diced

60 g (2 oz) chopped spring onion

2 teaspoons finely chopped garlic

2 tablespoons diced red onion

1/2 teaspoon finely chopped red chilli

2 tablespoons freshly chopped
   coriander

125 ml (4 fl oz) olive oil

1 tablespoon fish sauce

freshly ground pepper to taste

Cut the fish into large slices and season with calamansi juice, salt and pepper. Set aside for 15 minutes, then dredge in flour. Heat the oil until it starts to smoke, then lower heat slightly and fry the fish fillets until golden and crispy. Arrange on a serving platter.

Place the tomato, spring onion, red onion, garlic, chilli and coriander in a bowl, then add the oil and toss. Season with fish sauce and pepper and arrange over the fish.

Baked Stuffed Sole

INGREDIENTS | **SERVES 4**

4 sole fillets, 200 g (7 oz) each
1 tablespoon fresh lemon juice
salt and pepper
4 tablespoons cream cheese
2 teaspoons minced garlic
75 g (3 oz) Parma ham, shredded
100 g (4 oz) tomatoes, skinned,
   seeded and diced
2 tablespoons chopped fresh basil
75 g (3 oz) Mozzarella cheese,
   grated
fresh basil leaves

Lay the fillets on a flat surface and season with salt, pepper and lemon juice. Cream the cheese in a bowl, add the garlic and combine thoroughly.

Place a little ham, tomato, basil and Mozzarella cheese on each fillet and top with an even spread of the garlic cheese. Roll each fillet carefully to form tight rolls, then place on a lightly-buttered sheet of cooking foil. Wrap the foil like a parcel and carefully place on a baking tray.

Preheat an oven to Gas Mark 4 (180°C/350°F) and bake for 20 minutes, then unwrap the parcel, transfer the fish fillets to a warm serving platter and garnish with fresh basil leaves.

Mackerel in Garlic and Turmeric Sauce

INGREDIENTS | **SERVES 4**

4 mackerel steaks, approximately
150 g (5 oz) each
salt and pepper
2 tablespoons fresh lime juice
flour for dredging
125 ml (4 fl oz) cooking oil
3 cloves garlic, thinly sliced
2 tablespoons chopped onion
50 g (2 oz) shredded green and
   red pepper
2 teaspoons thinly sliced ginger
1 teaspoon ground turmeric
125 ml (4 fl oz) malt vinegar
2 tablespoons sugar
250 ml (9 fl oz) fish stock

Season the fish with the salt, pepper and lime juice, then dredge in the flour.

Heat 75 ml (3 fl oz) of the oil and pan-fry the fish until cooked, then remove and keep warm.

In a fresh pan, heat the remaining oil and fry the garlic until crispy. Remove and drain on kitchen paper. Add the onion, pepper and ginger to the pan and sauté for 3 minutes, then add the turmeric, vinegar, sugar and stock.

Bring to the boil, then lower heat and simmer for 5 minutes. Adjust the seasoning, add the fish steaks and continue to cook for a further minute until the fish is heated through, then transfer to a serving dish.

Dover Sole with Smoked Salmon Soufflé

Fillet the sole and remove the skin. Trim and season with salt, pepper and lemon juice. In a non-stick pan, heat the butter, add the thyme and then sear the fillets on one side only for 10 seconds. Allow to cool, then roll each fillet, seared side down, around your thumb and forefinger, leaving a 2 cm (3/4 inch) cavity. Secure with toothpicks and arranged on a buttered baking tray.

To make the soufflé, whisk together in a double boiler the butter, flour egg and milk and stir continuously over a gentle heat until the mixture thickens. Then, remove pan from heat, add the salmon, spinach, cheese, nutmeg and lemon juice and season to taste with salt and pepper. Beat the egg whites until stiff and, using a large spoon, gently fold into the spinach mixture.

Spoon a portion of the soufflé mixture into each fish roll. Preheat an oven to Gas Mark 4 (180°C/350°F) and bake the stuffed fish rolls for 10 minutes.

Meanwhile, to make the sauce, melt the butter over a medium heat and sauté the shallots and leeks until wilted. Add the Noilly-Prat and fish stock and reduce by half, then add the orange juice and tarragon and reduce again by one third. Finally, pour in the cream and simmer for 2 minutes, whisking continuously.

To serve, strain the sauce and spoon on to four individual dinner plates. Arrange 2 pieces of sole on each plate and garnish with the caviar, salmon roe and a sprig of tarragon.

Sole Parcels in Soy Broth

4 whole sole, 400 g (14 oz) each

salt and pepper

50 g (2 oz) plain flour

oil for frying

2 tablespoons shredded leek

1 tablespoon shredded ginger

2 tablespoons chopped coriander

1 Chinese cabbage

125 ml (4 fl oz) fish stock

1 tablespoon powdered dashi

2 teaspoons light soy sauce

1 teaspoon sesame oil

2 tablespoons sesame seeds, roasted

25 g (1 oz) shredded red pepper

25 g (1 oz) shredded leek

4 coriander sprigs

Scale and fillet the sole and season with salt and pepper. Combine the leek, ginger and coriander and season. Lay the fillets on a flat surface, spread with the vegetable mixture and fold in half.

Blanch the Chinese cabbage leaves and cut in half lengthwise along the rib. Discard the rib. Place fish sandwich in the middle of the leaf, fold over to enclose the fish and fold again to make a parcel, then steam for 5-7 minutes.

Bring the fish stock to the boil, then add the dashi powder and simmer for 2 minutes. Add the soy sauce and sesame oil, then remove pan from the heat.

Slice fish parcels in half diagonally and arrange on a serving plate. Top with sesame seeds, red pepper, leeks and coriander sprigs, then carefully pour the soy broth on one side of the plate and serve immediately.

Roasted Monkfish with Red Wine Sauce

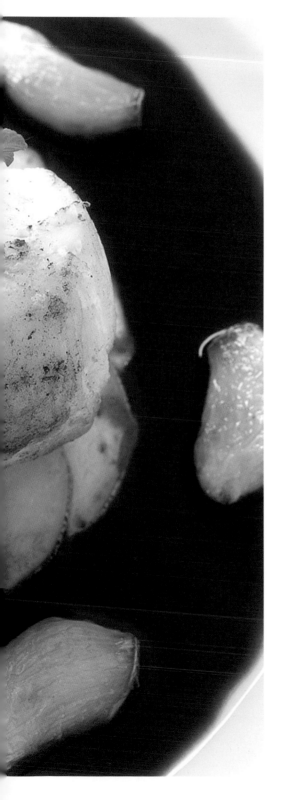

INGREDIENTS **SERVES 4**

4 monkfish fillets, 175 g (6 oz) each

salt and pepper to taste

2 teaspoons fresh lime juice

1 tablespoon French mustard

4 rashers streaky smoked bacon

3 tablespoons clarified butter

2 tablespoons olive oil

150 g (5 oz) courgettes, thinly sliced

1 tablespoon freshly chopped parsley

28 garlic cloves, peeled

2 tablespoons olive oil

RED WINE SAUCE

500 ml (18 fl oz) red wine

250 ml (9 fl oz) port

100 g (4 oz) unsalted butter, cubed

salt and pepper to taste

Season fillets with salt, pepper and lime juice and spread with a layer of mustard, then wrap a slice of bacon around each fillet.

Heat the butter in a pan and sear the fish on both sides, then transfer to a roasting tray. Preheat the oven to Gas Mark 4 (180°C/350°F) and cook the fish for approximately 8 minutes.

Drizzle the garlic cloves with a little olive oil, sprinkle with salt and pepper and wrap in foil, then bake in the same oven for 10 minutes. Season the courgette and place in a pan, add the chopped parsley, drizzle with the remaining oil, then toss over a moderate heat until the parsley is barely wilted.

To make the sauce, pour the red wine and port into a saucepan and bring to the boil. Reduce to just 75 ml (3 fl oz) and allow to cool slightly, then, over a low heat, add the cubes of butter, whisking briskly after each addition.

To serve, overlap the courgette slices in the centre of individual dinner plates. Place the fish on top and surround with the sauce and cloves of roasted garlic.

8 grouper fillets, 75g (3 oz) each
salt and pepper
1 tablespoon lemon juice
100 g (4 oz) plain flour
375 g (14 oz) clarified butter
2 tablespoons butter
4 bananas, sliced in half lengthwise
50 g (2 oz) sliced shitake mushrooms
250 g (8 oz) spinach, blanched
1 tablespoon chopped fresh parsley

250 ml (9 fl oz) fish stock
2 tablespoons finely minced ginger
2 tablespoons lemon grass,
 bulb bruised
2 tablespoons lemon juice
$\frac{1}{2}$ teaspoon lemon rind
100 g (4 oz) unsalted butter, cubed
100 g (4 oz) tomatoes, skinned,
seeded and diced

Grouper Caprice

The combination of fish and bananas is surprisingly delightful. The bananas here and in the following recipe must be a little under ripe so they remain firm after frying.

Season each grouper fillet with salt, pepper and lemon juice. Dredge in the flour and fry in the clarified butter until golden and crisp. Remove and keep warm. Add the bananas to the same pan and fry till soft, then set on one side and keep warm.

Heat $\frac{1}{2}$ tablespoon of butter and sauté the shitake mushrooms. Season, set on one side and keep warm. Heat the remaining butter and add the spinach. Season, set on one side and keep warm.

To make the sauce, pour the stock into a saucepan, add the ginger and lemon grass and bring to the boil. Reduce to half its volume, then strain and return to the pan. Continue to simmer for a few minutes, then add the lemon juice and rind. Add the butter cubes one at a time, whisking vigorously, then, just before serving, add the diced tomato.

Arrange the fish on a bed of spinach, top with the bananas and shitake mushrooms. Spoon the sauce around the plate and sprinkle with chopped parsley.

Fillets of Grouper with Bananas

8 fillets of grouper, 125 g (4 oz) each

1 tablespoon fresh calamansi juice

salt and pepper to taste

2 tablespoons flour

125 g (4 oz) clarified butter

4 small sweet bananas, halved
   lengthways

2 tablespoons shredded ginger

2 tablespoons shredded leek, green
   part only

RELISH

500 g (1 lb 2 oz) tomatoes, skinned,
   seeded and diced

2 tablespoons chopped onion

2 tablespoons minced garlic

3 tablespoons chopped fresh
   coriander

1 teaspoon finely chopped red chilli
   pepper

1 tablespoon shrimp paste

2 tablespoons olive oil

1 tablespoon fresh calamansi juice

freshly ground black pepper to taste

Season the fillets with calamansi juice salt and pepper. Dredge the fillets in the flour. Heat half the butter in a saucepan and fry the fillets for approximately 2 minutes on each side, until golden and crispy, then transfer to a warm serving platter.

Heat the remaining butter and fry the bananas until golden. Fry the ginger and leek until crispy.

Place the bananas alongside the fish and top with the crispy vegetables, then surround with the relish.

To make the relish, place all the ingredients in a bowl and combine well, cover with cling film and chill for at least 1 hour before serving.

4 turbot fillets, 175 g (6 oz) each
salt and pepper
150 g (5 oz) butter, softened
75 g (3 oz) chopped shallots
250 g (8 oz) button mushrooms
salt and pepper
1 tablespoon chopped parsley
750 ml (1½ pints) chicken stock
200 g (7 oz) chopped shallots
150 g (5 oz) whole morels
450 ml (16 fl oz) white wine
250 ml (9 fl oz) double cream
2 teaspoons fish curry powder
sprigs of fresh dill

Steamed Turbot with Morel and Curry Sauce

Season the fillets with salt and pepper. Melt 1 tablespoon of butter and use to brush the fish, then steam for 4 minutes.

Heat a further 3 tablespoons of butter in a saucepan and sauté the shallots. Remove the stalks from the button mushrooms and put to one side. Slice the caps and add to the shallots, then season, remove from the heat and stir in the parsley. Roughly chop the mushroom stalks and put in a pan with the chicken stock. Bring to the boil and reduce by one-third, then strain.

Heat the remaining butter and sauté the shallots, then add the whole morels and the mushroom broth. Cover and simmer gently for 20 minutes, then remove the morels and add the white wine and cream. Slowly reduce by half, then blend in the curry powder and adjust seasonings to taste.

To serve, place a portion of the mushroom mixture onto 4 individual plates and top with the fish. Pour the sauce around the sides of the plates and garnish with the morels and the sprigs of dill.

Tuna Steak with Mango and Tarragon

INGREDIENTS **SERVES 4**

800 g (1¹/₂ lbs) tuna loin

salt and pepper

2 tablespoons olive oil

2 mangoes, peeled and halved

125 g (4 oz) plain flour

1 egg, lightly beaten

75 g (3 oz) bread crumbs

1 tablespoon chopped chives

SAUCE

125 ml (4 fl oz) white wine vinegar

1 teaspoon chopped tarragon

75 ml (3 fl oz) chicken stock

2 eggs

salt and pepper

Tuna is the most versatile of fish, capable of being transformed with each change of accompaniment. With mango, this tuna is elevated to a really exotic dish.

Slice the tuna into 8 pieces and season with salt and pepper. Heat the oil in a pan and sear the tuna for 30 seconds on each side. Dredge mango pieces in the flour, dip in the egg and coat well with the bread crumbs, then deep-fry until golden brown.

To make the sauce, pour the vinegar into a pan and bring to the boil, then add tarragon and reduce the volume by half. Gently warm the chicken stock. Break the eggs into a fresh saucepan and place over a low heat. Whisk briskly while slowly adding the warm chicken stock. Continue until it becomes foamy, then, gradually blend in the vinegar reduction and season with salt and pepper.

To serve, ladle a little sauce onto 4 individual dinner plates, place 2 slices of tuna in the middle of each plate and top with mango. Garnish with chopped chives and serve immediately.

Tuna kebabs

INGREDIENTS SERVES 4

500 g (1 lb 2 oz) tuna loin
2 tablespoons fresh lime juice
salt and pepper
100 g (4 oz) red pepper
100 g (4 oz) green pepper
100 g (4 oz) yellow pepper
100 g (4 oz) leek
12 button mushrooms

DIPPING SAUCE

3 tablespoons vinegar
1 tablespoon light soy sauce
1 teaspoon chopped red chilli
1 teaspoon chopped spring onion
1 teaspoon crispy fried garlic

 Cut the tuna into 3 cm (1inch) cubes and place in a bowl. Season with salt and pepper, add the lime juice and set aside for 20 minutes. Seed the peppers and cut into squares. Cut the leeks into bite-size slices.

Lightly grease 12 skewers and thread on the tuna and vegetables in alternate layers, ending each skewer with a mushroom. Cook over charcoal, or under a hot grill, turning occasionally and serve on a bed of steamed rice. Combine all the sauce ingredients and serve on the side.

Red Snapper in Garlic Turmeric Sauce

INGREDIENTS SERVES 4

4 red snapper fillets, 200 g (7 oz) each

salt and pepper to taste

2 tablespoons plain flour

vegetable oil for frying

2 cloves garlic, slivered

2 tablespoons chopped onion

2 teaspoons minced ginger

50 g (2 oz) shredded green pepper

50 g (2 oz) shredded red pepper

1/2 teaspoon ground turmeric

100 ml (4 fl oz) vinegar

1 tablespoon sugar

100 ml (4 fl oz) fish stock

 Season the fillets with salt and pepper and dredge in flour. Heat 3 tablespoons of oil in a frying pan and fry until the fish is cooked, then drain on kitchen paper and keep warm.

Wipe the pan, add the remaining oil and sauté the garlic, onion, ginger and peppers and sauté for 2-3 minutes. Add the turmeric, vinegar, sugar and fish stock and bring to the boil, then lower heat and allow to simmer for 10 minutes.

Finally, adjust seasonings to taste, add the fish fillets and cook for a further minute, then transfer to a serving platter.

Baked Snapper with Peanut Pesto

INGREDIENTS SERVES 4

4 red snapper fillets, 200 g (7 oz) each
salt and white pepper
1 tablespoon fresh lime juice
30 g (1 oz) finely sliced onion
30 g (1 oz) finely sliced fennel bulb
30 g (1 oz) finely sliced carrot
30 g (1 oz) sliced thinly celery
30 g (1 oz) finely sliced leek
2 teaspoons olive oil
2 tablespoons chopped roasted
  peanuts
100 g (4 oz) tomato, skinned, seeded
  and diced
1 tablespoon chopped garlic
1 teaspoon freshly chopped
  fresh basil
2 tablespoons grated Parmesan
  cheese
75 ml (3 fl oz) olive oil
1 tablespoon butter, softened
2 tablespoons fish stock

Score the skin of each fish fillet with criss-cross slits, then season with salt and pepper and drizzle with lime juice. Toss the onion, fennel, carrot, celery and leek in the olive oil.

Grind the peanuts in a food processor, then add the tomato, garlic, basil and Parmesan cheese. Add the oil in a slow stream and adjust seasonings to taste.

Grease a piece of foil with the butter, add the fish fillets and top with the vegetables. Add the peanut sauce and the fish stock then fold the foil and seal tightly. Pre-heat an oven to Gas Mark 4 (180°C/350°F) and bake for 15-20 minutes.

Roasted Red Snapper

INGREDIENTS SERVES 4

2 kilo (4¹/₂ lbs) whole red snapper
salt and pepper to taste
juice of 1 lemon
2 tablespoons thinly sliced garlic
200 g (7 oz) diced onion
450 g (1 lb) tomatoes, skinned,
  seeded and diced
1 tablespoon fresh chopped thyme
3 tablespoons extra virgin olive oil
1 lemon, thinly sliced, seeds removed
3 tablespoons fish or chicken stock
3 tablespoons butter

This is one of the easiest of baked fish recipes. Snapper can be replaced by grouper or any firm fleshed fish.

Make diagonal slashes through to the bone in the thickest parts of the fish at 5 cm (2 inch) intervals. Season with salt, pepper and lemon juice.

Mix together the garlic, onion, tomato, thyme, olive oil and salt and pepper. Line an oven-proof serving dish with half the mixture and lay the fish on top. Insert the lemon slices into the slashes in the fish and cover with the remaining mixture. Pour on the stock, dot with the butter and cover with foil. Roast in a pre-heated oven at Gas Mark 4 (180°C/350°F) for approximately 30 minutes, then remove the foil and continue to cook for a further 10 minutes.

Red Snapper see previous page

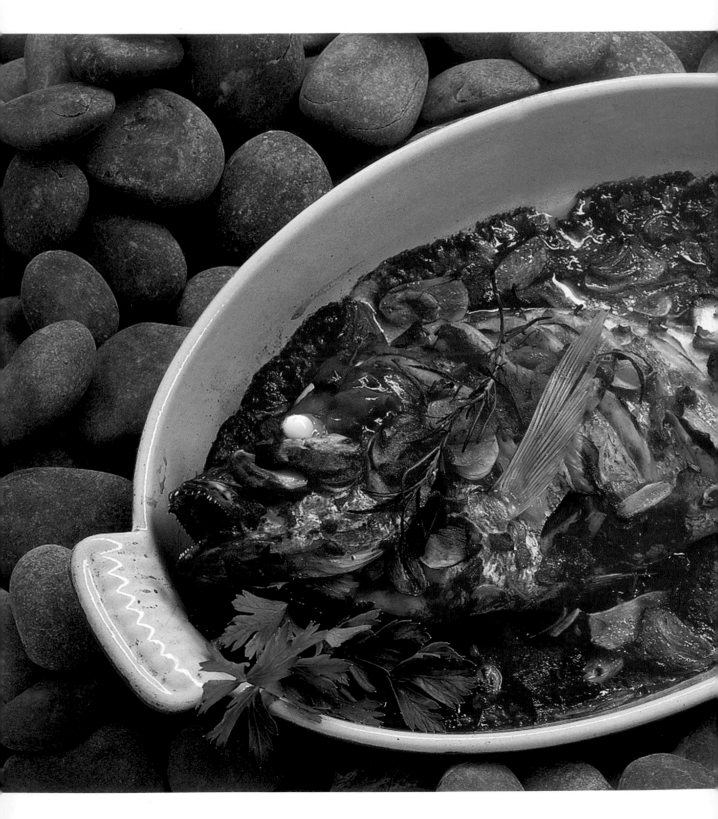

Stingray in Spicy Sauce

INGREDIENTS SERVES 4

350 g (12 oz) stingray (or skate) fillets

1 onion

1 stalk celery

1 bay leaf

1 teaspoon black peppercorns

3 tablespoons olive oil

1 tablespoon minced garlic

125 g (4 oz) onion, chopped

1 tablespoon chopped ginger

1 tablespoon chopped red chilli

125 ml (4 fl oz) vinegar

125 ml (4 fl oz) coconut cream

salt and freshly ground pepper

Blanch the fish in boiling water for 1 minute, then allow to cool and remove the skin. Bring 1.5 litres (2¼ pints) of water to the boil, add the whole onion, celery stalk, bay leaf and peppercorns and boil for 3 minutes. Add the fish and allow to simmer for a further 3 minutes, then remove the fish, scrape off the meat with a spoon and set to one side.

Heat the oil in a pan and sauté the garlic for 2 minutes. Add the chopped onion, ginger, chilli and vinegar. Simmer for 10 minutes, then add the stingray meat and cook for a further 2 minutes. Season to taste, add the coconut cream and bring to the boil, then remove from the heat and transfer to a serving dish.

Grilled Swordfish with Soy Onion Sauce

INGREDIENTS **SERVES 4**

4 swordfish steaks, 200 g (7 oz) each

salt and freshly ground black pepper

4 tablespoons fresh lime juice

75 g (3 oz) butter

200 g (7 oz) onion, sliced into rings

2 tablespoons light soy sauce

1 tablespoon oyster sauce

75 ml (3 fl oz) fish stock

1 tablespoon coarsely chopped
fresh coriander

Season the swordfish with salt and pepper and sprinkle with half the lime juice and leave for 15 minutes. Cook the fish under a hot grill, then transfer to a serving platter and keep warm.

Heat the butter in a frying pan and fry the onion rings until transparent, then remove and drain on kitchen paper. Add the soy sauce, oyster sauce and stock to the pan and bring to the boil. Simmer for 2 minutes, then replace the onion rings, add the coriander and remaining lime juice and cook for a further 30 seconds, then pour sauce over the fish and serve immediately.

Salt Cod Stew Brazilienne

This wonderful recipe was shared by a Brazilian friend whom
I met during one of my travels. The coconut cream spells the
difference in this salt cod stew; a different kind of creaminess
that brings to mind the tropical regions in another part of the world.

INGREDIENTS

500 g (1 lb 2 oz) salt cod
4 tablespoons olive oil
1 teaspoon minced garlic
3 tablespoons chopped onion
3 tablespoons chopped spring onion
1 red pepper, seeded and diced
1 green pepper, seeded and diced
3 bay leaves
200 g (7 oz) tomato, skinned,
  seeded and diced
125 ml (4 fl oz) fish stock
salt and pepper
125 ml (4 fl oz) coconut cream
2 tablespoons chopped green
  part of spring onion

 Soak the cod in cold water for 12 hours,
changing the water several times. Drain and
remove the skin and bones, pat dry and cut
into 5 cm (2 inch) slices.

Heat the oil in a saucepan and sauté the garlic, onion, spring
onion and peppers until the onion and peppers are soft.
Add the bay leaves, tomato, stock and cod. Cover and simmer
for 15 minutes, then season to taste. Stir in the coconut cream
and green spring onion pieces and heat through without letting
the mixture boil. Transfer to a large dish and serve immediately.

Eel Stewed in Garlic Soy and Vinegar

INGREDIENTS SERVES 4

1 kilo (2 1/4 lbs) fresh eel

2 tablespoons salt

1 tablespoon light soy sauce

1 tablespoon fresh lime juice

1 teaspoon freshly ground
   white pepper

200 ml (7 fl oz) sunflower oil

2 tablespoons minced garlic

125 ml (4 fl oz) vinegar

250 ml (9 fl oz) fish stock

3 bay leaves

 De-bone the eel and remove the head. Scrub wit the salt, then rinse in cold water. Cut the eel into serving size pieces and place in a bowl. Add the soy sauce, lime juice and pepper and set to one side for 30 minutes.

Heat the oil in a casserole and cook the eel for 2-3 minutes, turning to ensure the pieces are completely sealed, then remove and set aside.

Pour away most of the oil and sauté the garlic for 3 minutes, then add the remaining soy sauce, vinegar, stock and bay leaves and bring to the boil. Allow to simmer until the liquid has reduced by half, then replace the eel, cover the casserole and cook for a further 3-4 minutes.

Glossary

The following ingredients are listed as a helpful guide to preparing Asian style meals, such as those included in this book. However, where practical, more familiar alternatives have already been written in to individual recipes.

▌ Banana Heart

The male part of the banana, also known as banana flower. A maroon coloured sheath covers the flesh, which is usually sliced and used in salads or added to soups or sauces.

▌ Banana Leaves

Often used to wrap stuffed dishes because they are so readily (and cheaply) available throughout Asia. They certainly add an authentic touch but, if difficult to find, aluminium foil is perfectly suitable.

▌ Calamansi

This small citrus fruit is a hybrid of the mandarin and kumquat and is used frequently in Philippine cooking to add a slightly sour taste. It is seldom found outside that country and limes make the best substitute. Calamansi mixed with soda plus a dash of sugar syrup makes a very refreshing drink.

▌ Coconut Milk

The milk is made from the grated flesh of a mature (brown) coconut being squeezed with water. On average the flesh of one coconut squeezed with 75 ml (3 fl oz) of water will produce a thick milk, or cream. In Asia this is generally known as the first pressing. Adding extra water to the flesh and squeezing again, the second pressing, will produce a thin milk. Where fresh coconuts are not available the cream and milk are readily available, frozen, dried or in cans, at most supermarkets.

The 'milky' liquid inside a young (green coconut) is known as coconut water and is often used in soups. It also makes a very refreshing drink.

▌ Coriander

Also known as Chinese parsley. The leaves, chopped or whole, are generally added towards the end of the cooking process or else used as a garnish. The seeds, whole or ground are frequently pounded with other ingredients to produce spice paste.

▌ Dashi

A Japanese soup stock, made from dried fish and seaweed, available in dried or liquid form from most Asian provision stores

▌ Fennel

The leaves and seeds add a slightly aniseed flavour and go particularly well with fish.

▌ Fish Sauce

A salty brown sauce with a strong flavour. There are a number of varieties, some more pungent than others, but it should always be used sparingly

▌ Grouper

A family of fish found widely in the seas around Australia and South East Asia. Cod, or other firm flesh white fish can well be substituted.

▌ Lemon Grass

An aromatic grass with a small bulbous root which, when crushed, adds a strong lemon flavour, which goes particularly well with both shellfish and fish dishes. Best fresh but, if unavailable, the powdered variety, often sold commercially as serai, makes an acceptable substitute.

▌ Milkfish

A herring-like fish abundant throughout the Pacific. It has a soft white flesh with a delicious taste but has the disadvantage of having many small bones. It is quite difficult to catch and now cultivated in fish farms, particularly in the Philippines, where it is regarded as a great delicacy.

▌ Mirin

A sweetened sake (Japanese rice wine) only used in cooking. A dessert wine or a sweet sherry could be substituted. Quantities used depend on personal tastes.

▌ Morels
Mushrooms with a distinctive honey-comb body. They are difficult to cultivate and as a result are not widely available and so relatively expensive to buy fresh. However, they are available dried or in cans.

▌ Palm Sugar
A hard brown sugar made from the juice of the coconut plain flower. Generally crush or grated before using to add a sweet balance to an otherwise sour dishness

▌ Pompano
A firm fleshed sea water fish abundant in the waters around South East Asia the Caribbean.
If unavailable can be replaced with sole or plaice.

▌ Sesame Oil
A strong oil with a slightly nutty flavour made from roasted sesame seeds. Small quantities will enhance the flavour when used in cooking or in side dips. It is not used as a cooking oil.

▌ Shrimp Paste
A paste with an extremely pungent aroma. Most commonly sold in small slabs, although liquid variety is also available. Should always be used sparingly.

▌ Tamarind
The tree is native to East Africa but well established in Asia. The pods contain small beans which are made into a pulp, then dried. The pulp can be reconstituted in warm water and added to a dish to provide sourness.

▌ Turmeric
Although the root is available in many Asian markets it is generally sold and used as a powder. Has very little taste but adds an attractive yellow colour to sauces.

▌ Wasabi
A herb used to produce a pale green paste usually referred to as Japanese horseradish. A little mixed with soy sauce provides a strongly flavoured dip, ideal with many fish dishes. Can be bought as a powder and reconstituted in a little water or vinegar.

▌ Water Chestnut Flour
A flour used mainly for thickening. Cornstarch can be substituted.

▌ Wonton Wrappers
Squares of very thin dough made with a high glutinous flour. Readily available in Chinese food stores and often found frozen in many Western supermarkets. They are used to encase a variety of fillings for snacks or soups.

Weights and Measures
The foregoing recipes have been written using metric measurements, grams (g) and milliliters (ml), with approximate Imperial measures, ounces (oz) and fluid ounces(fl oz), shown in brackets. For accurate conversion the nearest whole unit is 28:1. Wherever practical small quantities are given in teaspoons (5 g/ml) and tablespoons (15g/ml).

Index